The John Amos
Conference Cen
in Rackova Dol

Retirement home
ZVOLEN

Pavel SINKO Lucenec
Mission-worker and
Church Planter

International Needs
Slovakia

SLOVAKIA
The Heart of Europe

My Slovakia,
Land of my fathers,
You're beautiful like paradise...

SLOVAKIA
The Heart of Europe

Oľga Drobná
Eduard Drobný
Magdaléna Gocníková

Bolchazy-Carducci Publishers, Inc.
Wauconda IL, USA

PERFEKT

Bratislava, Slovakia

Slovakia: The Heart of Europe

English edition of *Slovensko moje*, published by PERFEKT,
Karpatská 7, 811 05 Bratislava, Slovak Republic, in 1996
Translated by: Martin Clifford Styan, Zuzana Paulíková
General Editor of the English Edition: Alexander MacGregor, Ph.D.

First English edition is published by

PERFEKT

Bolchazy-Carducci Publishers, Inc.
1000 Brown St., Unit 101
Wauconda IL 60084, USA

Karpatská 7
811 05 Bratislava
Slovak Republic

ISBN 0-86516-318-7

ISBN 80-8046-037-X

Printed in Tlačiarne Banská Bystrica, Slovak Republic, 1996

Library of Congress Cataloging-in-Publication Data

Drobná, Oľga.
    (Slovensko moje. English)
    Slovakia, the heart of Europe / Olga Drobna, Eduard Drobny, Magdalena Gocnikova.
      p. cm.
    Includes bibliographical references.
    Summary: An overview of a European country of great natural beauty, emphasizing its rich cultural traditions.
    ISBN 0-86516-319-7 (alk. paper)
    1. Slovakia--Juvenile literature. (1. Slovakia.) I. Drobný, Eduard. II. Gocníková, Magdaléna.
III. Title.
    DB2711.D7613 1996
    943.73--dc20

                                              96-25905
                                                CIP
                                                    AC

This is where we were born, this is our native country. The land will not disappoint anyone who loves it. This is our home where we can always return. This is where people who understand and love us live.

You have to know your home and see it. You have to learn everything that's beautiful and special about it. You have to know everything you can be proud of, everything that distinguishes our home from other countries.

This book is dedicated to everyone who was born here and also to those who have never seen the country of their grandfathers and fathers, to all those who live all around the world and may sometime return to Slovakia, the way one returns home. Learn how to love your native country with the help of this little book.

Legend about Slovakia and the Slovaks

The Wealth of the Slovak Nation

The great spiritual wealth of Slovakia has been preserved in legends, fairy tales and stories, as well as in folk songs. Grandchildren learnt them from their grandmothers, so they could be kept alive until the present.

People had already forgotten the flood, and had grown in number until they became so numerous that they could no longer live in the old country. When there were too many of them and they couldn't live in the old country the Lord told them to go throughout the world. He didn't leave them with empty hands; He gave every nation a special language and special treasure. It was very lively and busy when all the nations met in front of the Lord's throne, where the Lord gave them the presents they were asking for:

"Lord, give us fertile land which has plenty of milk and honey!"

"Lord, give us strength and power so we can rule over other nations!"

"Lord, give us splendor and glory so we can become famous throughout the world!"

And the Lord gave away everything he had.

And here are the Slovaks at the very end going to meet the Lord.

They walk very respectfully, but there are only a few of them, the fewest of all.

"Welcome my children. Why are you coming last?"

"O Father, forgive us, but the bigger nations pushed us aside and it would be in vain to push a little nation up to the front."

"Well, what shall I give you? The greater nations have already got the lands, power and glory."

"We ask neither for great lands nor for power or glory; we ask you only for one thing. We only want your love."

"So you want love, the greatest gift of all? If you want love, you shall have it and I shall love you, the Slovak nation, forever!"

And the Lord is smiling, smiling at the Slovaks just as a father smiles at his children because he likes their request the most.

But where are the limits of the Lord's generosity? Who could ever reach its bottom?

So he puts his finger into the well of Paradise and touches the Slovaks´ tongues, and says:

"I am giving you the most beautiful language in the whole world. The Slovak language will sound like the singing of the angels. It will be as beautiful as the dew shining in the sun. The Slovak language will be as pleasant as a breeze in May, as sweet as a baby comforted by its mother, as nice as the smile of an innocent child. Listening to its sounds, the hearts of young and old alike will grow younger!"

He turns for the second time to the well of Paradise and takes from it the most beautiful songs, puts them into Slovak mouths, and says: "I am also giving you the most beautiful songs. If your women start to sing, the birds will fall silent, the brooks will start sparkling, and hills will jump a little. The singing of your women will turn your country into a paradise!"

And the Lord smiles for the third time and says all good things come in threes:

"And I am giving you a beautiful land under the Tatras, which will be your home. That's where you will work in your fields, that's where you'll raise your families, that's where you'll keep the Christian faith and the Slovak language. And even if you suffer, do not give up: for I shall remember you with a Father's heart and I shall always help you!"

"Oh, thank you, good Lord, thank you that you didn't forget the Slovak nation!"

And so the Slovaks have been living under the Tatras in their fathers' country for more than a thousand years, and will stay there forever because the Slovak nation serves God and God always protects them.

THE SLOVAK REPUBLIC
The heart of Europe

Slovakia has a special location. Almost in its geographical center, in a village called Krahule near Kremnica (latitude 48° 44' north and longitude 18° 55' east), there is the center of Europe itself.

Try to spread love and friendship and mutual understanding from this country in the center of Europe to the other countries of the world.

BOW YOUR HEAD TO HONOR ITS FLAG

Czech Republic

Poland

Ukraine

Austria

Hungary

The Slovak national anthem

There is Lightning on the Tatras

Lyrics by Janko Matuška ● music: folk song

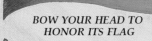

Nad Tatrou sa blýska, hromy di-vo bi-jú. Nad Tatrou

sa blýska, hromy di-vo bi—jú, zastavme ich, bratia,

ved'sa o—ny stratia,Slováci o-ži—jú. Slováci o-ži-jú.

There's lightning on the Tatras,
the wild thunder roars!
There's lightning on the Tatras,
the wild thunder roars!
Let us stop it, brothers!
Look, it's disappearing!
The Slovaks are reviving!
The Slovaks are reviving!

8

BRATISLAVA - capital of the Slovak Republic

We can trace the history of this ancient town back into prehistory. Prehistoric and early historical castles and settlements were built in the place where the great European river ´the Danube´ meets the Carpathian Mountains, to the east of the Alps. This is where two European plains meet: the Vienna and Komárno basins. This is the reason why Bratislava was an important crossroads of military and trade routes even in ancient times. These routes were used by many ethnic groups of different cultures and religions. The most important were the Celts, who built a prehistoric town or *oppidum*, at the end of the last millennium before Christ. During the Great Moravian Empire, Bratislava Castle was one of the most important strategic, governmental and administrative centers; later it became a seat of the religious and civil administration of the Kingdom of Hungary. The nearby Devín Castle was also important in the time of Great Moravia. Bratislava was granted town privileges in 1291 by King Andrew III.

At the beginning of the 16th century, at the time of the Turkish invasions of Central Europe, the Kingdom of Hungary joined the Habsburg Monarchy; and Bratislava became its capital city. Bratislava was the seat of the Hungarian aristocracy, administrative center and meeting place of the Hungarian Parliament.

In 1563, Maximilian II became the first King of Hungary to be crowned in Saint Martin's Cathedral in Bratislava. He was already King of Bohemia and in 1564 he became Holy Roman Emperor, that is, overlord of the whole of Central Europe. During the next 300 years, ten kings and one queen – Maria Theresa – were crowned in Saint Martin's Cathedral. Eight wives of kings were also crowned queen there. The last coronation was that of Ferdinand V in 1830. The last Hungarian parliament was held in Bratislava during the revolution of 1848. This assembly was very important for Slovak history because the Slovaks were represented in it by Ľudovít Štúr who made a famous speech defending Slovak rights.

Bratislava has almost half a million inhabitants. It is the seat of the Slovak President and government institutions, such as the National Council of the Slovak Republic or Parliament, the Government of the Slovak Republic, ministries, embassies and other important offices. Thousands of Slovak and foreign students study at the Bratislava universities – Comenius University, the Slovak Technical University, the University of Economics, the Academy of Fine Arts and Academy of Performing Arts.

Important national cultural institutions are concentrated in Bratislava: the Slovak National Theatre with its operas as well as dramas, New Stage Theatre (Nová Scéna), Astorka Theatre (Divadlo Astorka), the Slovak Philharmonic Orchestra, the folk dance group Lúčnica and the Slovak Folk Art group (SĽUK), the Slovak National Gallery, the Slovak National Museum, the Slovak Radio, Slovak TV and many others. Thanks to many well-known artists, the Slovak cultural message reaches the world.

Bratislava is also the seat of the Slovak Academy of Science and scientific institutions, which represent Slovak science at home and abroad.

There are many more professional and amateur theatrical, dancing and singing groups performing and working in Bratislava and Slovakia.

The Sights of Bratislava

1. Devín Castle - A strategic fortress, on a site inhabited since the late Stone Age. During the Great Moravian Empire it was a defensive fortress of Prince Rastislav. In 1809 it was destroyed by Napoleon's army.

2. The Slovak National Theater - a neo-renaissance building constructed in 1884-1886 as the town theater. Since 1920, it has served the needs of the Slovak National Theater. In front of the main entrance is the famous Ganymede Fountain.

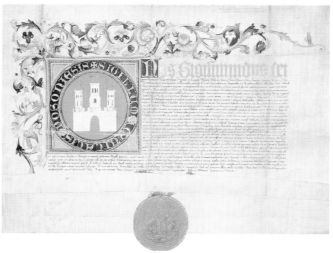

Charter bearing a coat of arms granted to Bratislava by King Sigmund in 1436

3. The Old Town Hall - the oldest in Slovakia. It already served this purpose in the 14th century, when it was not the town's property but the private house of the town's mayor, Jacob.

4. Grassalkovič Palace - built in 1765 for the head of the administration of the Kingdom of Hungary, Prince Grassalkovič. It is now the seat of the President of Slovakia.

5. The New Bridge - a unique suspension bridge. The bridge was built in 1973 as the second bridge over the Danube at Bratislava. Today there are four bridges in Bratislava.

6. House of the Good Shepherd - a Rococo style building from 1760. It is a precious remnant of what used to be perhaps the most picturesque street in Bratislava, with nice little shops. The rest was demolished to make room for the approach road to the New Bridge.

7. The Castle is the dominant feature of the Bratislava panorama. It has been of strategic importance since time immemorial. During the Great Moravian Empire the castle was one of the most important administrative centers. The present buildings are basically 15th century, but with many later reconstructions and additions. The castle was most important in the 16th century, when the Turks occupied Budapest, and Bratislava became the capital of the Kingdom of Hungary. A fire of 1811 left the castle in ruins for the next 150 years. The restoration in the 1960's gave the castle its present form. Today one section is used for state occasions and another is open to the public as part of the Slovak national Museum.

8. Michael's Gate - the only survivor from the four gates in the fortifications of the old town, which originated in the 13th century. It acquired its present form in the 18th century. The five storey square tower is a dominant feature of the pedestrian area of the old town.

9. Saint Martin's Cathedral - a Gothic church of the basilica type, with side aisles the same height as the central part. It was built in the 14th and 15th centuries on the site of an older Romanesque church. Over almost 300 years, the church was used for the coronations of kings of Hungary. The golden crown, which is placed on a pillow at a height of 85 meters, reminds us of this significant function of the church. The sculptor Juraj Rafael Donner made a famous statue of St. Martin for the church in the 18th century and designed the interior of the Chapel of St. John the Almsgiver.

10. The Primacial Palace - a beautiful neoclassical building from the 18th century built as the seat of the Archbishop of Esztergom. It was the finest house in the town. In 1805, a peace treaty between Napoleon and the Emperor of Austria was concluded there after Napoleon defeated Austria at the Battle of Austerlitz. There is a valuable collection of tapestries from the 17th century and a unique hall of mirrors. The courtyard contains a fountain with a 17th century statue of St. George killing the dragon.

Great Moravia

The area of modern Slovakia was settled by Slavs at the end of the 5th century. At the beginning of the 7th century, the Slavs were attacked by the Avars, a nomadic tribe from the Eurasian steppes. The peaceful Slavs resisted under the leadership of a Frankish merchant called Samo who defeated the Avars.

After his death the empire broke up; but the Slavs were never pushed out of the area. They lived in peace with their southern neighbors, the Avars. The destruction of the Avar Empire around the year 800 made it possible for independent Slav states to rise in its place. The Principality of Moravia, centered around the modern Slovak-Czech border, was led by Mojmír, while the Principality of Nitra in western Slovakia was ruled by Pribina.

After 833 Mojmír added the Principality of Nitra to his own and created an independent state, the Great Moravian Empire. Mojmír was followed by Rastislav as the ruler of Great Moravia. Louis the German, King of the Eastern Franks, in what is now Germany, did not like the independence and success of the new state, so he attacked it and took advantage of the ambitions of Rastislav's nephew, Svätopluk, who governed the Principality of Nitra. In 870, Svätopluk betrayed Rastislav and handed him over to the enemy, who imprisoned and blinded him. But Svätopluk was soon paid back for his treason when King Louis the German accused him of hostility to his son Karolman and put Svätopluk in prison as well.

With the help of lies and intrigues, Svätopluk got out of prison, placed himself at the head of a strong army of Slavs and defeated Karolman's army.

Svätopluk became a strong and feared ruler of Great Moravia. He recovered its independence, defended it against invaders and extended its frontiers. Under Svätopluk Great Moravia reached the peak of its power and territorial extent. It included not only the greater part of Slovakia and Moravia, but also modern Bohemia and parts of Hungary and Poland. Well-developed industry and trade, culture, literature and education placed Great Moravia among the most developed states in Europe at that time.

Rastislav - ruler of Great Moravia. He invited the Thessalonian brothers Constantine-Cyril and Methodius to teach Christianity in Great Moravia.

Pribina - Prince of Nitra, later of Pannonia (modern western Hungary). Around 828, he consecrated the first Christian church in Slovakia.

Mojmír - Prince of Moravia, who united the principalities of Moravia and Nitra about 833 to form Great Moravia. He ruled until 846.

12

Saint Cyril and Saint Methodius - Byzantine teachers of the Christian faith.

Odra

Morava

Váh

Hron

Tisza

Svätopluk I - ruler of Great Moravia from 871 to 894

Gorazd - disciple of Methodius

Drava

Dunaj

Stars in the Slovak Sky

Every nation honors its forefathers. Those of the Slovaks include no fighters or leaders who exterminated smaller nations, destroying their towns and culture. The Slovaks were a peaceful, hard working and religious people who always proudly defended their rights against more powerful nations.

Jozef Maximilián Petzval (1807-1891) – physicist, mathematician, inventor, founder of modern photography.

Štefan Banič (1870-1941) – inventor. He invented the first parachute, which was used in the First World War.

Wolfgang Kempelen (1734-1804) – inventor of a typewriter for the blind, and the famous chess-playing automaton.

Maximilián Hell (1720-1792) – mathematician, astronomer. He was the first to calculate the distance between the Earth and the Sun.

Samuel Mikovíni (1686-1750) – cartographer, maker of the first maps of Slovak regions and head of the first mining school in Europe - The Mining Academy in Banská Štiavnica.

Jozef Murgaš (1864-1929) – theologian, one of the pioneers and inventors of wireless telegraphy.

Ján Andrej Segner (1704-1777) – world-famous German scientist who was born in Bratislava. He designed a steam turbine.

Andrej Kmeť (1841-1908) – historian, archeologist, theologian and botanist. He tried to prove that the Slovaks are the original inhabitants of the Kingdom of Hungary.

Matej Bel (1684-1749) – scholar called "a great adornment of Hungary" for his learning. He was the founder of modern geography in the Kingdom of Hungary.

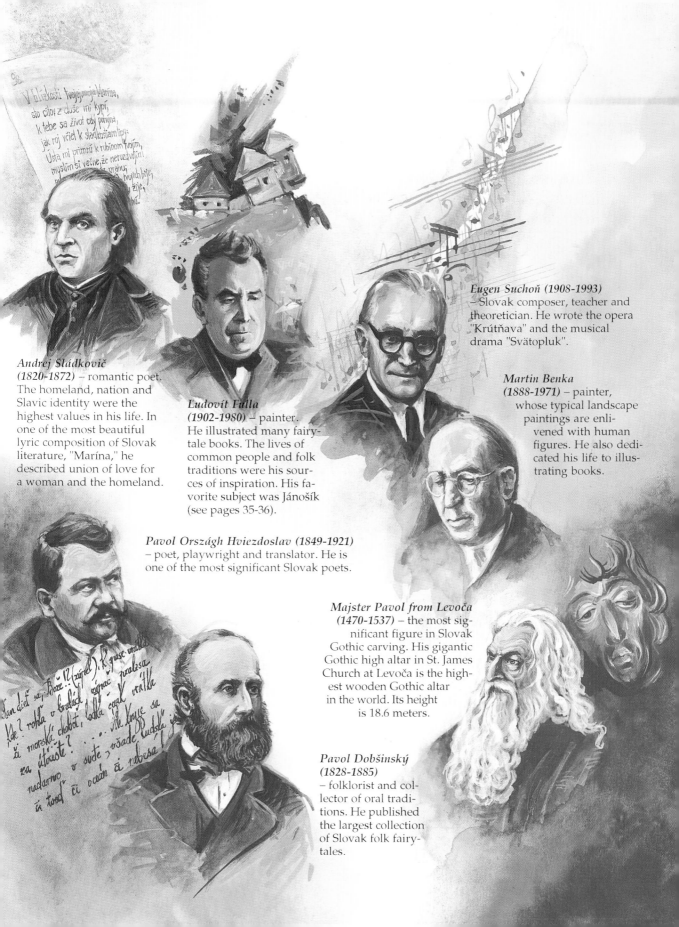

Andrej Sládkovič (1820-1872) – romantic poet. The homeland, nation and Slavic identity were the highest values in his life. In one of the most beautiful lyric composition of Slovak literature, "Marína," he described union of love for a woman and the homeland.

Ľudovít Fulla (1902-1980) – painter. He illustrated many fairy-tale books. The lives of common people and folk traditions were his sources of inspiration. His favorite subject was Jánošík (see pages 35-36).

Eugen Suchoň (1908-1993) – Slovak composer, teacher and theoretician. He wrote the opera "Krútňava" and the musical drama "Svätopluk".

Martin Benka (1888-1971) – painter, whose typical landscape paintings are enlivened with human figures. He also dedicated his life to illustrating books.

Pavol Országh Hviezdoslav (1849-1921) – poet, playwright and translator. He is one of the most significant Slovak poets.

Majster Pavol from Levoča (1470-1537) – the most significant figure in Slovak Gothic carving. His gigantic Gothic high altar in St. James Church at Levoča is the highest wooden Gothic altar in the world. Its height is 18.6 meters.

Pavol Dobšinský (1828-1885) – folklorist and collector of oral traditions. He published the largest collection of Slovak folk fairy-tales.

Not every nation has to fight for its borders, for its mother tongue, for the right to its own existence. The small Slovak nation had to win all these fights, and it took hundreds and hundreds of years.

Often, those who attacked or settled in Slovakia tried to erase the beautiful Slovak language from the minds of the people. They tried to make the Slovaks speak Hungarian. Earlier, they had encouraged the use of German or Latin. Then the borders changed and they said that Slovak was only a Czech dialect. Who were they?

Larger nations, which did not acknowledge the Slovak identity, perhaps thought that the Slovaks just needed to be annexed to another country. But they did not succeed. Past generations of Slovaks had to fight hard so there would always be a place for Slovakia. Slovakia´s friends abroad also tried their best in the fight.

For example, the Norwegian writer Bjornstjerne Bjornson supported Slovakia's right to self-determination at of beginning of the 20th century, and helped us unselfishly with all his strength. He did this because he loved our country and believed that even a small nation has the right to its own life and democratic development.

Well-educated people who are interested in the people, their language, culture and economic development are important for every nation. The Slovaks have many forefathers who attempted to do that. The most important people who tried to raise the Slovak language and national consciousness set an example for us.

In the last third of the 18th century, national consciousness grew together with the need for a literary language. *Anton Bernolák (1762-1813)*, a Catholic priest, undertook this important task. His proposal called "Bernolákovčina" was based on the west Slovak

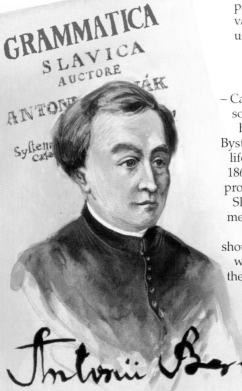

Štefan Moyses (1796-1869) – Catholic priest , professor of philosophy, well-known spokesman for his people, was Bishop of Banská Bystrica from 1851. He dedicated his life to educational development. In 1861, he played a prominent role in protests against the treatment of the Slovaks by the Hungarian government, and argued that all nationalities in the Kingdom of Hungary should have equal rights. He was the first chairman of the Slovak cultural association, Matica Slovenská.

16

dialect. Anton Bernolák created a phonetic spelling (written as pronounced). He explained his system in his Slovak grammar (*Grammatica slavica*) in 1790.

Further development occurred in Slovakia, and an agreement on the codification of the Slovak language as a written language was reached in 1843 at Hlboké, near Senica in West Slovakia. Ľudovít Velislav Štúr, Jozef Miloslav Hurban and Michal Miloslav Hodža were especially concerned with codifying the Slovak language. As the basis they chose the central Slovak dialect, which they thought was the purest. In the new literary language *Ľudovít Štúr (1815-1856)* also used phonetic spelling.

These reforms were accepted with enthusiasm, especially by young people, and in 1844 the first publications in literary Slovak appeared.

Martin Rázus (1888-1937) – a Protestant clergyman, prominent politician, national activist and writer. He was an opponent of Magyarization (the effort to make the Slovaks speak Magyar or Hungarian) and national repression. After the establishment of the Czechoslovak Republic, he opposed the idea of one Czechoslovak nation. He wrote books for children called *Maroško* and *Maroško studies*.

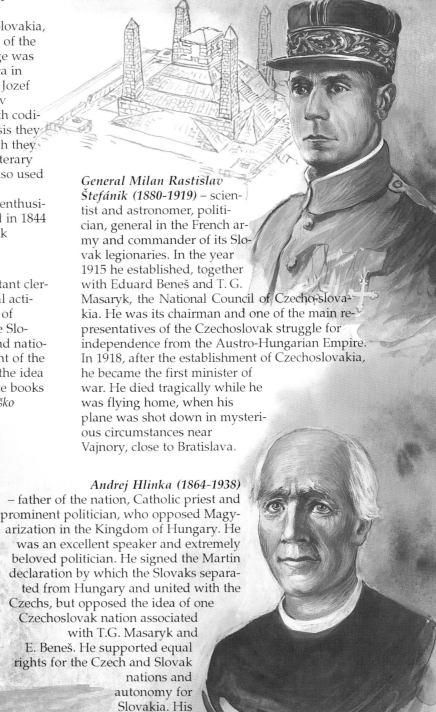

General Milan Rastislav Štefánik (1880-1919) – scientist and astronomer, politician, general in the French army and commander of its Slovak legionaries. In the year 1915 he established, together with Eduard Beneš and T. G. Masaryk, the National Council of Czecho-slovakia. He was its chairman and one of the main representatives of the Czechoslovak struggle for independence from the Austro-Hungarian Empire. In 1918, after the establishment of Czechoslovakia, he became the first minister of war. He died tragically while he was flying home, when his plane was shot down in mysterious circumstances near Vajnory, close to Bratislava.

Andrej Hlinka (1864-1938) – father of the nation, Catholic priest and prominent politician, who opposed Magyarization in the Kingdom of Hungary. He was an excellent speaker and extremely beloved politician. He signed the Martin declaration by which the Slovaks separated from Hungary and united with the Czechs, but opposed the idea of one Czechoslovak nation associated with T.G. Masaryk and E. Beneš. He supported equal rights for the Czech and Slovak nations and autonomy for Slovakia. His place of burial is unknown.

The Slovak Cultural Association

MATICA SLOVENSKÁ

Karol Kuzmány

The first Slovak cultural institution was established in August 1863. From its establishment to its suppression by the Hungarian government in 1875 it was the only Slovak cultural institution.

Without any state support and dependent solely on the gifts of the Slovak people, it developed broad activities. The institution had an academic function and published the first Slovak academic periodical, called the *Annals of the Slovak Cultural Association*. The association organized cultural activities and published books and calendars. It laid the foundations of national science, libraries, archives and museums. It became a symbol of the unity and survival of the nation. Its leaders were prominent religious representatives. The chairman of the Slovak Cultural Association was the Catholic bishop Štefan Moyses, and the first deputy chairman was Karol Kuzmány, a leading Protestant.

After the suppression of the Slovak Cultural Association, the institutions established by it continued to work on the association's activities. After its reestablishment in 1919, the Slovak Cultural Association was led by literary and cultural historians and public figures. Jozef Škultéty became its

Jozef Škultéty

Štefan Krčméry

Jozef Cíger Hronský

lifelong administrator. But the greatest contribution to the Slovak Cultural Association came from the administrative work of the writer Jozef Cíger Hronský, who had to emigrate in fear for his life in 1945. In the 1950s, the Slovak Cultural Association could not develop independently, so he established in 1959 a Slovak Cultural Association abroad. Since 1954 the association has been a state academic institution with responsibility for the Slovak national library. The association is also building up libraries, archives and museum collections. It runs the central archives for literature and an art and literature museum. The association cooperates with Slovaks living abroad and publishes academic literature.

Cover of the by-laws of the Slovak Cultural Association

After the revolution in November 1989 the association was reformed, its executive bodies were elected and the association participates in the life of society. Under the law of the Slovak Parliament from 1991, " The Slovak Cultural Association is a national, cultural and academic institution with the task of supporting national activities within Slovakia and abroad. To carry out this task, the association cultivates love of the homeland and supports the moral and cultural life of the Slovak nation. The association links the creators and supporters of Slovak culture and helps its development; it protects and develops the national heritage as well as national and cultural values."

Slovaks in the World

Slovaks live not only in their homeland, in the country under the Tatra Mountains; you can meet them all around the world as well. There are 1.5 million Slovak-speaking people in the rest of the world.

Emigration because of scarcity and unemployment started in the 17th century. Today about 500,000 Slovaks live in Hungary, the former Yugoslavia, Poland, Rumania and the Czech Republic, but the biggest waves of emigration were directed towards America and Canada. About one million Slovaks live there today. There are also about 5,000 Slovaks living in Australia and even in Africa. The Slovak language is taught in 17 countries and at 30 universities. The descendants of the emigrants need to have a tight

Emblem of the Slovak World Congress

connection with their ancestral homeland, as do the Slovaks who remain at home. The Slovak Cultural Association provides Slovaks abroad with books and magazines, and organizes meetings and folk performances for them. It

strives to be a spiritual mother to them.

The Slovaks living abroad are organized in the Slovak World Congress, which was established in New York in 1970. Several years before the establishment of the Congress, Štefan Boleslav Roman, a Slovak living in the US, submitted a proposal to Slovak organizations all over the world to unite and create an institution. The role of the Slovak World Congress is to speak for Slovaks in the world, to represent them, protect their interests and spread the good reputation of the Slovaks.

The World Congress pays attention to young Slovaks living abroad, and since 1980 it has been organizing world meetings of Slovak youth.

1. Bratislava

- the capital of the Slovak Republic is also called the *Belle of the Danube*. Its dominant historic feature is the Castle, which looks like a table upside-down.

2. Devín

- the remains of an ancient castle overlooking the point where the River Morava flows into the Danube. Near the castle is the state nature preserve called Devínska Kobyla, which means Devín mare. On Devínska Kobyla you can find rare species of plants and animals. It is the only place in Slovakia where the rare *Rhamnus saxatilis* and all the species of the *Ophrys* orchid still grow. This is the home of our biggest spider, *Lycosa singoriensis*, and a great number of insects.

3. Modra

- old royal borough situated in the Little Carpathian Mountains. It is well-known for its delicious wine and beautiful pottery. A white base and multicolor flower ornaments are very typical of Modra pottery. Ľudovít Štúr lived here from 1851 until he died in 1856. He is buried in Modra.

4. Trnava

- the "Slovak Rome". This name arises from the many churches and monasteries which were built in and around Trnava. In 1238, Trnava became the first town to be awarded the rights of a free royal town. From 1635 to 1777 Trnava was also a university town. In the 18th century it became a centre of Bernolák's activities in raising the national consciousness.

5. Červený Kameň (Red Stone)

- a great castle near Modra. We know from writings that a castle already existed here in 1240. After the restoration, the castle became a museum of historical furniture. The interior has rich painted decoration from the 17th century done by Italian artists.

6. Skalica

- since the 6th century the town area has been settled by a Slavic population. On Calvary Hill we can find the Romanesque rotunda of St. George and the remains of a nobleman's seat from the 12th and 13th century. These are national cultural monuments. Skalica today is a modern printing center; it also produces good red wine called Skalica ruby and special round cakes.

7. Bradlo

- the highest mountain of the Myjava Hills (543m/1780ft). On the top of the mountain there is a monument to General Milan Rastislav Štefánik, a significant figure in Czechoslovak history. The monument was designed by the famous Slovak architect Dušan Jurkovič.

8. Gabčíkovo

- a massive dam and hydro-electric complex on

Places of

28. Vychylovka

26. Tercho

16. Čičmany

15. Trenčín

17. Trenčianske Teplice

27. Br

14. Moravany nad Váhom

18.

6. Skalica

13. Piešťany

12. Topolčianky

5. Červený Kameň

7. Bradlo

11. Tesárske Mlyňany

19. B
Stia

2. Devín

3. Modra

4. Trnava

10. Nitra

20. Dua

1. Bratislava

8. Gabčíkovo

9. Komárno

Morava

Váh

Interest

Podzámok

31. *Vysoké Tatry*   32. *Ždiar*   45. *Červený Kláštor*   46. *Bardejov*

30. *Zuberec*

Orava

47. *Bardejovské kúpele*   55. *Drevený kostol v Jedlinke*

38. *Paludza*   44. *Vyšné Ružbachy*   48. *Spišský hrad*   54. *Veľká Domaša*   53. *Brekovský hrad*

9. *Liptovská Mara*

línec

33. *Kežmarok*

34. *Ganovce*

Hornád

37. *Čierny Balog*

36. *Demänovská jaskyňa*

35. *Dobšinská ľad. jaskyňa*

43. *Levoča*

52. *Zemplínska Šírava*

23. *Korytnica*

Ondava

Laborec

40. *Detva*

50. *Herľany*

Bystrica

42. *Krásna Hôrka*

49. *Košice*

51. *Poznasovce*

21. *Zvolen*

Bodrog

41. *Domica*

the world. The Hungarian writer Mor Jokai and the Austrian composer Franz Lehár were born at Komárno.

10. Nitra
- an important Slovak town with a rich history, one of the centers of the Great Moravian Empire. Around the year 820 Prince Pribina consecrated the first church in Slovakia in Nitra. Today, Nitra is a modern town with two universities, part of the Slovak Academy of Sciences and a well known exhibition place called the Agrokomplex.

11. Tesárske Mlyňany
- a village in the valley of the River Žitava known for the Mlyňany Arboretum, a park containing many exotic plants and trees. It was established in 1892 by Štefan Ambrózy Migazzi. In 1951 it was declared a state nature preserve. Today it belongs to the Slovak Academy of Sciences.

12. Topoľčianky
- a village near Nitra. The original fortress from the 15th century was reconstructed and transformed into a neoclassical mansion surrounded by an English-style park. Since 1918 the castle has been a summer seat of the Czechoslovak presidents. Topoľčianky is also known for its horse and bison breeding.

13. Piešťany
- the location of a famous spa already known in the 16th century. The first mention of its medicinal springs dates from 1545. The

the River Danube which brought life back to old tributaries of the Danube. Experts call it a project for the third millennium. The constructions prevent floods, make the Danube river navigable, produce electricity and create a great vacation resort. The village of Gabčíkovo was first mentioned in 1264. The emperor Franz Jozef I was born there.

9. Komárno
- an ancient town, situated where the rivers Danube and Váh join, and already a significant port in the 11th century. The castle from the 12th century was rebuilt and in 17th century became the best bastion against the Turks in the Kingdom of Hungary. Ships are built there and used throughout

spa treats mainly illnesses of the joints. The symbol of the town is a healed man breaking his crutch.

14. Moravany nad Váhom
- a village in the district of Trnava, where archeologists found a Paleolithic (Early Stone Age) statue known as the "Moravany Venus". It is the oldest work of art from Slovakia.

15. Trenčín
- an important town located in the Váh Valley. A text carved into the rock of the castle hill by the Romans in 179 A.D. is the oldest example of writing in Slovakia. It

includes the word "Laugaritio," the name of the village from which the town of Trenčín developed. The most important period in Trenčín's history was the 14th century, when the Trenčín Castle was a seat of Matúš Čák, a noble who ruled much of Slovakia for a time.

16. Čičmany
- a little village in the district of Žilina. Since 1977, it has been a museum of folk architecture. One or two storey wooden houses with shingle roofs and ornaments painted on the

wood are very typical of the village. Even today, all the folk traditions are preserved here.

17. Trenčianske Teplice
- in the 16th century this spa was already considered one of the most important in the Kingdom of Hungary. The thermal water has excellent properties for treating rheumatism and neurological disorders.

18. Kremnica
- a famous old gold mining town. The town became famous for its mint, which is one of the oldest in the world. It was established in the 14th century, producing the silver groš, and the gold florin or Kremnica ducat for the Kingdom of Hungary. It produced most of Hungarian coins until 1918, and then Czechoslovak coins until 1992. Today it makes the coins of the Slovak Republic. Commemorative medals have also been produced since the 16th century.

19. Banská Štiavnica
- an old mining town with well-preserved Renaissance architecture. The town was awarded town privileges in 1241. Silver in particular was mined here. The mining technique was on a very high level. Gunpowder was used here for the first time for mining. In 1762 the Mining Academy, first mining

college in Europe, was established here. The town is on the UNESCO list of the world cultural heritage.

20. Dudince
- a spa where the hot springs have excellent properties for healing illnesses of the joints and digestion problems. There are many archaeological sites in the district.

21. Zvolen
- the old commercial and cultural center of the Zvolen basin. Thanks to its strong fortification, it withstood the Turks.

22. Banská Bystrica
- an important town in the Zvolen basin since the 13th century, the town is situated at an important crossroads of trade routes. The town also was and still is the center of the political, national and cultural life of Central Slovakia. It is the home of Matej Bel University and was the center of the Slovak National Uprising against Nazism in 1944.

23. Korytnica
- a spa established next to therapeutic springs in the 19th century to treat diseases of the digestion and metabolic disorders.

24. Vlkolínec
- a little village near Ružomberok with traditional wooden houses and other well-preserved historic buildings. Since 1993, the village has been on the

UNESCO list of cultural monuments.

25. Martin (Turčiansky Sv. Martin)
- a well-known trade and manufacturing town. In the 14th century the town was given the right to hold a market. Later Martin became the center of Slovak national activities. In 1861 a national assembly issued a resolution calling on the Hungarian Parliament to give the Slovaks autonomy and equal rights with the other nationalities in the Kingdom. Martin is the seat of the Slovak Cultural Association; and its national cemetery is the final resting place of important Slovak figures.

26. Terchová
- the home town of the hero Juraj Jánošík still retains its traditional spirit, with its folk costumes, carved dishes, songs, dances and folk stringed instruments.

27. Budatín castle

- a castle situated where the rivers Kysuca and Váh join. The castle was established in the 13th century as a frontier fortress at a major intersection of trade routes. Today it is a unique museum of tinkers and their metalwork.

28. Vychylovka
- museum of Kysuce village. There are open air museums of typical Slovak villages at several places in Slovakia. Houses, churches and other buildings which cannot be retained in their original locations are brought to these museums from the whole of Slovakia. The museum of Kysuce village is one of them. A special feature of Vychylovka is a steep railway six miles long which has been submitted for inclusion in the UNESCO list of the world cultural heritage.

29. Oravský Podzámok
- a village where perhaps the most beautiful castle in Slovakia is situated. Many generations left the poverty of Orava to find work in different parts of the world.

30. Zuberec
- a village which was established in the 16th century. Typical wooden houses with shingle roofs are preserved there. An open-air museum of folk architecture from Orava is located here.

31. Vysoké Tatry - the High Tatras
- the most compact concentration of mountains of Alpine character in the world, and the only ones of their kind in Slovakia. The Tatras provide great downhill and cross-country skiing opportunities, with ski jumps and slide routes as well.

32. Ždiar
- a picturesque village below the Tatras with well-preserved houses and folk traditions. The village is a place visited by lovers of tradition, beauty and relaxation.

33. Kežmarok

- there was a prehistoric settlement on the site of the town. In the 14th century, Kežmarok was made a royal town. In the 19th century, the secondary school in Kežmarok played a great role in the development of Slovak education. Much Renaissance architecture is preserved in the town. A wooden church built without a single nail also has historical and cultural value.

34. Gánovce
- a village in the Poprad district where the fossil skull of a Neanderthal man was found. It is the oldest evidence of people living in Slovakia. The oldest evidence of the use of iron in Central Europe also comes from Gánovce.

35. Dobšinská Ľadová Jaskyňa
- its ice cavern was discovered in 1870 and was the first in Europe to have electric lights. It was the place where Slovak ice skater Karol Divín practiced. He won a silver medal at the Olympic Games in 1960.

36. Demänovská Jaskyňa Slobody
- the "Cavern of Liberty," located in the Low Tatras. The cavern was discovered in 1921 and is the most visited and the most beautiful of the 30 caverns located in the Demänovský Kras.

37. Čierny Balog
- a village in the valley of the Čierny Hron river. Its area also contains the Dobročský Natural Forest. The village was established in the 16th century, a time when other wood-cutting villages were established in an area which received the name Čiernohorský region (Black Forest region). A narrow-gauge forest railway was built here at the beginning of the 20th century. During the Second World War, the village was the scene of fighting against the Nazis.

38. Paludza
- this village already existed in the 12th century but has been flooded by the Liptovská Mara reservoir. The beautiful wooden church was removed to the village of Lovisko.

39. Liptovská Mara
- a reservoir on the River Váh between the towns of Liptovský Mikuláš and Liptovská Teplá. The construction of the reservoir began in 1969 and was finished in 1975. It is one of the biggest man-made lakes in Slovakia.

40. Detva
- a jewel of folk culture and Slovak spirit, with its houses, countryside, wood carving, especially of the unique musical instrument called *fujara* (a long pipe) and painted and carved wooden crosses. The Slovak poet Andrej Sládkovič was inspired by the region while writing the poem *Detva*. For the last three decades folk festivals have been held there.

41. Domica
- a cavern known since 1926, which was formed by the action of underground water. The cavern was inhabited in the Later Stone Age. The cave is part of a system which extends into Hungary.

42. Krásna Hôrka
- a medieval castle situated above the village of Krásnohorské Podhradie near Rožňava.

Today a museum and gallery are located in the castle. The graves of the noble Andrassy family lie under the castle.

43. Levoča
- from the 13th century one of the the most important trade and manufacturing centers in

Slovakia. In the 16th century, paper production and printing were already established in Levoča. In the mid-19th century, the Levoča Lyceum played a major role in the development of Slovak national culture. The main altar in St. James Church, created by Master Paul at the beginning of the 16th century, is a unique art work of world importance. Levoča is a much-visited place of pilgrimage.

44. Vyšné Ružbachy
- a spa with mineral hot springs was already established in the 15th century. Neurological diseases, illnesses from work, and blood pressure problems are treated here. There is also a travertine quarry, with an open-air museum of sculpture. International symposia on sculpture are held here.

45. Červený Kláštor (Red Monastery)
- a complex of medieval buildings from the 14th century. The monasteries of the Carthusians and Camaldolesians are national cultural monuments. Brother Cyprian, a famous Camaldolesian monk who lived here, collected medicinal plants and published an herbal based on them. In the beautiful national park of Pieniny rafting remains a major attraction on the River Dunajec.

46. Bardejov
- a rich old trade town, which in the 15th century was one of the largest in Slovakia. In 1581 the first book in the Slovak language was printed here. In 1986, Bardejov was awarded a European prize and a gold medal for restoring its historical buildings and monuments. Beautiful Gothic and Renaissance buildings are preserved in the town.

47. Bardejovské Kúpele
- springs of iron-rich mineral water provide healing treatments of the digestion and respiratory systems. There is also an open-air museum of folk architecture.

48. Spiš Castle

- one of the largest castles in Central Europe, it is open to visitors and is on the UNESCO list of the world cultural heritage. In the nearby village of Spišský Štvrtok, the lords of the castle of the Zápoľský family built a Gothic chapel in 1473. It is one of the finest Gothic churches in Slovakia.

49. Košice
- metropolis of East Slovakia and an important town since the 13th

century. The town is dominated by the 15th century church of St. Elizabeth, the largest Gothic building in East Slovakia and an important national cultural monument. A university and its press were established here in 1657. Košice became a center of cultural life and it is an important crossroads with well-developed industry and a rich scientific and cultural life.

50. Herľany
- has been known since the 17th century for its mineral springs. It is also famous for its geyser, a unique phenomenon in Central Europe. Its height varies from 70 to 200 feet and the water temperature is 73°F (23°C).

51. Pozdišovce
- a village already known in the 15th century for its well-developed pottery and ceramic. The village is known for its pottery even today. The typical design is a figured pattern on a black background.

52. Zemplínska Šírava Reservoir
- also called the sea of Eastern Slovakia, it was being built from 1962 to 1967. Today it is a popular vacation resort.

53. Brekov Castle

- was built in the second half of the 13th century on the site of an older castle. It is one of the oldest castles of Zemplín.

54. Veľká Domaša Reservoir
- an artificial lake built between 1962 and 1967. The lake serves as a vacation resort and also for hydro-electric production.

55. Wooden church in Jedlinka
- a national cultural monument. The church displays the skill of the Slovaks in using natural material.

The Well at Rastislav's Devín

Just as families preserve stories of their old and famous members, nations also hand down stories of ancient times from generation to generation, by oral tradition. Here is one of them.

From year to year Devín and its castle were growing, with more and more new buildings going up. A palace for Prince Rastislav and other buildings were built with wood from the surrounding forest. A wide, deep moat with a high rampart strengthened by a palisade of logs defended it on one side, the rivers Morava and Danube on the others. In times of danger, all the people of the district could crowd into it, along with everything they could carry.

They were safe there but lacked water, and people cannot live without water. And so a castle without a well is not really a castle.

It was sad at Devín. The rock was hard. There was no rain, and it was so terribly dry that the great rivers, Danube and Morava, almost dried up. Nobody could drink from them, there was no

water in the cisterns, and the rock had no pity. It was necessary to dig into it by force.

"Let's start digging!" said Rastislav to encourage them. "If we only dig a hole the size of my hand each day, we'll still have a well sooner than if we only look bewildered at each other and wait for a miracle to happen."

They listened to him. The rock gave off sparks under the blows of the men, and the pit quickly got deeper and deeper. The sounds of digging resounded from underground. Joy spread through the castle and moistened the drying lips of the suffering people. But then something happened which nobody expected. The men who were digging the well began to disappear. Whoever went down the hole never came up again. And since no-one returned, no one knew where the men had gone.

The Prince proclaimed to the country that whoever solved the mystery of the well would be richly rewarded. Many gallant lads and strong men came, but none of them came out of the well.

When all the attempts failed, the Prince had the well covered

with beams. He did not want anyone else to think of looking into it and trying his luck in battle with a pitiless fate.

"Perhaps it will get better," people comforted themselves. "Maybe it won't last forever." But instead of improving, times got worse. The sun was so hot that the earth cracked and the rivers dried up completely. There was not even a drop of water in the cisterns. Even the springs in the mountains stopped flowing.

In these desperate times, when almost every day somebody died from thirst or from illness caught from the dirty water of the rivers and swamps, the brave young Duke Slavoboj, son of the lord of the castle of Šintava, came to Devín. He came to show his admiration for Miloslava, daughter of the prince of Devín. She was like a rosebud opening early on a sunny morning.

"Everything would be fine, if only we had a well!" said Rastislav to Slavoboj in a friendly conversation.

Slavoboj became silent and began to think about it. He also thought about the well when he walked with his noble fiancée in the wide castle courtyards. He was still reflecting on the mystery of the well when he stopped at the beams which covered it.

He put his hand to his forehead to wipe away the sweat and to drive away the thoughts which had given him no peace since he arrived at Devín, and drove him to the well to test his luck, courage and skill. They put the idea into his head that he would succeed where the others had failed. He had to prove himself to his bride, and show whose hands she was entrusting herself to. He looked at Miloslava, he looked at the well, and remembered those who had gone into it and never came out.

But suddenly he noticed on the ground a strip of fresh grass. Not a strip, not a cross either, but a sword. Yes, a sword. The strip of green grass had the shape of a sword.

"Look, a sign for me! I must fight and try my luck!" he said.

He scraped away the grass and before him was a sword which only a giant could take in his hands. He lifted it, cleaned it, fingered it, tested it. He felt a strength and resolution in his body such as he had never felt before.

"Go", he said to his fiancée, "call your parents, armor-bearers and the whole household. Something strange will happen, something which has never happened here before."

At first the girl was surprised and didn't know what he meant. But when she saw where his eyes were looking, she was scared and wanted to ask him not to go into danger. She wanted to tell him that she would rather live without water but with him than with

water but without him. She wanted to speak but didn't because she perceived that she would disturb him deep in his thoughts.

Miloslava rushed away; soon the lord of the castle with his armor-bearers, household and people from the village of Devín came. They all knew Slavoboj. They had already heard much about the heroic deeds by which he had distinguished himself at Šintava, where he guarded the crossing of the River Váh. They were curious about what courageous deed he was going to do now. When they saw him by the well, they immediately knew what he was planning.

Some of them tried to dissuade him, saying that he should not test the Lord God and should think of Miloslava. If anything happened to him, she would never find another support like him. Perhaps she would also get ill and die, and there would be not one but two very precious lives on his conscience. But nothing could dissuade Slavoboj. He tied a strong rope round himself and lowered himself into the hole which should have been a well but wasn't. When Miloslava saw him leave the ground and hang onto the rope, she cried: "For the love of God, don't let him go down that hole!" Then she collapsed into the arms of her frightened mother. The people became quiet, fearing something unheard of. And when the armor-bearers put back the beams over the hole, it seemed that the heroic young man was already buried. From below came only the silence of the grave, which sank into their trembling hearts.

But not for long. After an hour, or perhaps after only half an hour, such a cracking and banging was heard from there, as if somebody were fighting. Heavy groans and firm blows resounded. Nobody knew who was giving them. Then there was complete silence once again. It was broken only by the painful sobbing of Miloslava, who had regained consciousness. Everyone was frightened. They thought that Miloslava saw her fiancé through the beams and the rocks, and mourned for him. "It's already over!" someone whispered, "and what a pity!" But then he signaled. Who else could have made the three blows of the sword on the hard rock? Only he. It was a pre-arranged sign for the armor-bearers to pull him out. As soon as they heard, they leapt to the well, took away the beams and pulled the strong ropes. Hope revived. Again everybody looked curiously at the well; again they hardly dared to breathe. They waited to see who would appear. In those strange times, anything could happen. First the sword appeared, then Slavoboj's head, and finally the whole hero.

He said nothing and only smiled. When they helped him to his feet, he swayed and fell down again. He was so exhausted and injured, that it was as if he had been struggling with Hell itself. But the main thing was, he still lived and breathed.

The princely family knelt down by him and endeavored to revive him. While the Princess and Miloslava caressed him and breathed over him, calling on him gently, he opened his eyes

and smiled. Meanwhile, the Prince concerned himself with something else.

Under Slavoboj's garment he found the bloody and hideous head of a strange creature. He took it out and looked at it. Now he knew where the men had disappeared, when they dared to go down the well. A dragon had devoured them. Perhaps they had penetrated his lair, but failed to escape. Well, praise God, Slavoboj had put an end to him. "You won't harm anyone else!" said Rastislav to the bloody head of the terrible monster, and he hurled it to ground so strongly that it dug into the rock. And behold, from the pit which it hollowed out sprang a strong current of pure water. Devín was saved. But nobody bent down to refresh his parched lips, when

close to them in weakness and fever lay the man who had saved them. Everyone gave way to Miloslava, who took water in her hands to refresh the mouth and forehead of her beloved. While she revived him, deacons, baptized and taught by the holy Father Methodius, began to sing a hymn of thanks to God, who had shown mercy to the suffering and given drink to the thirsty. Slavoboj was the most beloved man in Devín. They wreathed him with garlands because of the glory of his heroism, by which he had freed the people of Devín and its surroundings from the curse. And it was a wedding to end all weddings.

As long as Slavoboj and Miloslava lived, there was water in the well, but when they both died, on the same day, the

"dragon's well" suddenly dried up. But God had not forgotten the people of Devín. At the same moment a new well opened in the castle. And the water in it was just as healthy and refreshing.

Although Slavoboj died and the dragon's well became dry, the miraculous sword of the heroic Slavoboj remained. After many hard wars, it returned to the well, and awaits a hero who will take it up and strike the enemy with it, when the Slovaks need it most.

Vladimír Plicha
Ján Domasta
Slovak Historical Legends

Ornaments of the Slovak Landscape

Castles, mansions, and manor houses add to the beauty of Slovakia. They are a romantic background to our country, evidence of the skill of our people, monuments to its rich history and former glory, as well as sites for archeological research. Many of them are accessible to the public and much visited.

The castles, mansions and manor houses were built from the 12th to 19th centuries; and many legends, stories and veils of mystery are woven round them. The map shows only a handful of them. If you travel through Slovakia in any direction, sooner or later you will see one.

Let us approach some of them:

8. Strečno Castle

6. Trenčín Castle

3. Červený Kameň

5. Čachtice Castle

7. Bojnice Castle

11. Kremnica Town Castle

2. Devín Castle

4. Nitra Castle

1. Bratislava Castle

1. Bratislava Castle

The oldest traces of human activity on the site go back to four thousand years before Christ. The oldest building on the site was a stone church from the end of the 9th century.

After 1542, Bratislava was the capital city of the Kingdom of Hungary, and meetings of the Hungarian parliament were held in the castle. The castle was often reconstructed and adapted to contemporary needs. The last and greatest reconstruction was done in the time of the Empress Maria Theresa. The exteriors and interiors of the whole castle area were renovated. The castle has magnificent halls and museum collections. Part of it is open to the public.

2. Devín Castle

Devín Castle is the oldest castle in Slovakia. Its site was already inhabited in prehistoric times. At the time of Great Moravia, it was called Dowina; and two smaller hill-forts near Devínska Nová Ves also belonged to it. Devín is a symbol of Slavic brotherhood and the struggle of the Slovaks for freedom and national independence. In the first half of the 19th century, Ľudovit Štúr and his supporters revived its glory by organizing regular trips to Devín.

3. Červený Kameň

The original castle, built as a frontier fortress, was first mentioned in 1240. Today, a massive castle stands on a spur of the Carpathians. It is an important specimen of castle architecture. This imposing building, comparable to the best fortresses in Central Europe, acquired its present form

– Castles and Mansions

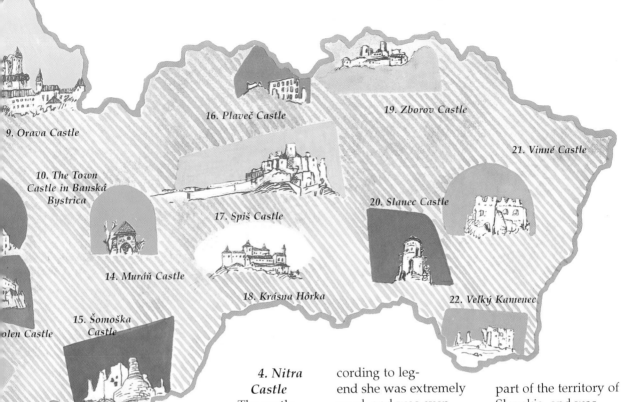

9. Orava Castle

10. The Town Castle in Banská Bystrica

16. Plaveč Castle

17. Spiš Castle

14. Muráň Castle

18. Krásna Hôrka

15. Šomoška Castle

olen Castle

rý kameň

19. Zborov Castle

21. Vinné Castle

20. Slanec Castle

22. Veľký Kamenec

in the middle of the 16th century, when the Fuggers demolished the original building and constructed a Renaissance fortress, which served as a base for trade. Then the Pálffys owned the castle until 1945. The castle is open to the public. The richest collection of interior furnishings in Slovakia is found here.

4. Nitra Castle
The castle was built on the site of an older Celtic-Dacian and Slavonic hill-fort. The area inside the castle contains the Cathedral, really three adjoining churches of the Romanesque, Gothic and Baroque periods. The castle is still the seat of the Roman Catholic Bishop of Nitra.

5. Čachtice Castle
This castle is associated with many legends woven round the figure of the Lady of Čachtice, Elizabeth Báthory. Ac-

cording to legend she was extremely cruel, and was even said to have preserved her beauty by bathing in the blood of young women. Čachtice Castle was part of a system of 13th century frontier castles along the River Váh. Only ruins survive.

6. Trenčín Castle
Trenčín Castle is splendidly situated on a high hill overlooking the old town center and valley of the River Váh. Its most important lord was Matúš Čák, who became Count Palatine in 1296. He ruled a large

part of the territory of Slovakia, and was called the Lord of the Váh and the Tatras. The beautiful story of the love of Omar and Fatima is associated with the castle. Omar rescued his beloved from captivity by cutting a well into the castle rock and forcing the rock to give up its water. The castle is open to the public and contains a museum.

7. Bojnice Castle
Documents show that the castle already existed in 1113; and a reference to hot springs is

one of the first from Slovak territory. The

castle underwent its greatest renovation at the end of the 19th century, when it was owned by Ján Pálffy.

Today Bojnice Castle, with its fairy-tale beauty, is one of the most visited; and its romantic appearance leads to it being used by foreign film makers.

The park around the castle contains the oldest linden tree in Slovakia.

8. Strečno Castle

"There around Strečno, a dangerous way" they sing in a folk song, because the Váh below Strečno was often the scene of rafting accidents. Strečno dominates the road from Žilina to Turiec. The castle was destroyed in 1698 by order of the Emperor after a rebellion. The ruins witnessed the first battles of the Slovak National Uprising in 1944. The castle is again accessible after the extensive restoration work.

9. Orava Castle

One of the most picturesque Slovak castles stands on a steep rock 112 meters above the River Orava. It was built to guard the route to Poland, and is first mentioned in 1267. It is divided into upper, middle and lower parts. Archeological finds show that the site was already settled about 1000 B.C. In spite of being damaged by fire in 1800, the castle (thanks to restoration) is one of the best preserved in Slovakia.

10. The Town Castle in Banská Bystrica

In some towns in Slovakia, separate fortified quarters were formed from various buildings. The town castle here had a defensive function and is today a national cultural monument. The oldest building is the parish church of the Assumption of the Blessed Virgin Mary. It is partly Romanesque, but was later reconstructed as a large Gothic church. There were several later alterations. The fortifications included four bastions. The entrance gate incorporates a barbican and the so-called pretorium, later used as the town hall, built about 1500.

11. Kremnica Town Castle

The irregular four-sided town square is overlooked by the complex of buildings of the Kremnica town castle. It was entered through a bastion, which is still preserved. The complex dates from the 13th to 15th centuries.

12. Zvolen Castle

It was built in the 14th century, outside the boundaries of the town, according to the model of the Italian type of castle. It served as a royal summer residence and base for hunting. It was reconstructed many times. In the 20th century, the last restoration aimed to uncover the whole complex and preserve valuable details. It serves the public for cultural purposes.

13. Modrý Kameň

The original stone castle originated in the 13th century. In the 15th century, a Gothic mansion was built in the lower part of the castle, which fell before the attacks of the Turkish army in the 16th century. In the first third of the 18th century, an Italianate manor house was built in the lower part of the castle. Today only the ruins survive, but the visitor is rewarded with a fine view.

14. Muráň Castle

The highest situated and one of the largest castles in Slovakia was first mentioned in 1271. It extends over a high hill in the Revúca Valley. The castle is surrounded by extensive woods, and flocks of sheep graze below the castle. The castle changed owners and after 1609 belonged to the Séči family. The most famous inhabitant of the castle was the beautiful Mária Séčiová, known as the Venus of Muráň. The castle burned down in 1702. Only ruins of the original Gothic castle remain at the top of the hill.

15. Šomoška Castle

This little castle lies squarely on the Slovak Hungarian frontier, near Fiľakovo. It was built in the 14th century and for one and a half centuries shook under the attacks of the Turks. Today only ruins remain. It is interesting that in building it basalt was used from under the hill. This breaks up into hexagonal prisms.

16. Plaveč Castle

The castle was built in 1294 as a frontier fortress. It frequently changed owners and was repeatedly reconstructed. Today only the high walls of the residential wing and the ruins of the castle keep the visitor fascinated.

17. Spiš Castle
This is the largest castle complex in Central Europe. In spite of the fact that the first written mention of it dates from the 13th century, it is clear that the castle was built much earlier. Research shows that the oldest tower was built around the year 1100. The castle hosts an exhibition documenting the prehistoric and medieval settlement of the castle rock and the history of military techniques. Parts of the castle have been restored and conserved. The castle, one of the most visited in Slovakia, is popular with film companies because of its remarkable position and appearance.

18. Krásna Hôrka
The castle contains rooms with period furniture. Below the castle is the Mausoleum in which the beautiful and legendary wife of Dionýz Andrassy is buried.

The story is told that the castle was built by a poor shepherd called Bebek. Bebek, who tended his sheep on a hill, once found a treasure – a huge jewel and a pot full of coins. The shepherd went to the King and gave him the jewel as a present. When the King wanted to reward him, Bebek asked if he could keep the coins which he found in the pot, and build seven mountain huts. The King gave permission, and the clever Bebek built seven castles. When the King came for a visit after some time, he rewarded Bebek and named the castle on the hill, the Beautiful Hill (*Krásna Hôrka*).

So much for the legend. The reality is that the castle was built after 1318 by the Mariáš family to guard an important road from Gemer to Spiš. The Bebek family acquired it in 1352, and extended the castle according to an Italian fortification system.

19. Zborov Castle (older name: Makovica)
Although this castle has been in ruins since 1684, when the imperial army captured and destroyed it, its surviving walls demonstrate the skill of people who built it. The first mention of the castle dates from 1347. It was built to guard a route from the Kingdom of Hungary to Poland. After 1364, the castle belonged to the Cudar family, who treated their peasants in a cruel and inhuman way, which led to frequent rebellions.

20. Slanec Castle
This may be the most picturesque ruined castle in East Slovakia. The first mention of it dates from 1281, but a hillfort probably stood on the site long before that. After the beginning of the 17th century it belonged to the Forgáč family. In 1644, it was gutted by fire, and damaged further later in the century; but it was still partly rebuilt and kept up. The last restoration was done by Jozef Forgáč, who made the castle tower into a family museum. The tower is still preserved today.

21. Vinné Castle and Manor House
The ruins of this castle stand on a southern spur of the Vihorlat Mountains, overlooking the Zemplínska Šírava Reservoir. Formerly it guarded a trade route to Poland. Historical sources do not mention this castle, but archeologists have dated it to the 13th century. It was destroyed by the beginning of the 18th century. A late Renaissance manor house from the 17th century is still preserved in the village of Vinné.

22. Veľký Kamenec

In the southernmost part of Zemplín, near the Hungarian frontier, stand the ruins of this castle, which bear witness to the varied and difficult past of this region. The village of Kamenec was mentioned for the first time in 1283. The castle was built after the Mongol invasion. Jan Jiskra and Ján Hunyady signed a peace treaty here in the 15th century. In 1672, the king ordered the destruction of the castle because the owner had participated in a rebellion.

THE HIGH TATRAS

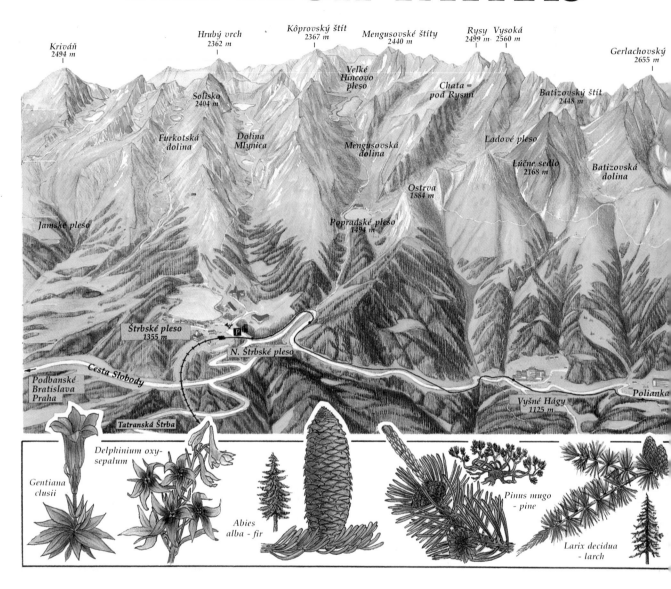

Kriváň 2494 m
Hrubý vrch 2362 m
Kôprovský štít 2367 m
Mengusovské štíty 2440 m
Rysy 2499 m
Vysoká 2560 m
Gerlachovský 2655 m
Solisko 2404 m
Veľké Hincovo pleso
Chata pod Rysmi
Batizovský štít 2448 m
Furkotská dolina
Dolina Mlynica
Mengusovská dolina
Ladové pleso
Lúčne sedlo 2168 m
Batizovská dolina
Ostrva 1884 m
Jamské pleso
Popradské pleso 1494 m
Štrbské pleso 1355 m
N. Štrbské pleso
Cesta Slobody
Podbanské Bratislava Praha
Vyšné Hágy 1125 m
Polianka
Tatranská Štrba

Gentiana clusii
Delphinium oxy- sepalum
Abies alba - fir
Pinus mugo - pine
Larix decidua - larch

The High Tatras, along with the Belianske Tatras, are the single Alpine mountain range, not only in Slovakia, but in the whole of the Carpathians. The main ridge is just 16 miles (26.5 km) long and 11 miles (17 km) wide. It begins at Ľaliové Sedlo and ends at Kopské Sedlo.

The highest peak of the Tatras is Gerlachovský Štít with a height of 8,710 feet (2,655 m). The western part of the High Tatras is dominated by Kriváň, which is known as the most beautiful mountain in Slovakia, and is a symbol of national pride. It is 8,180 feet high (2,494 m).

Thousands of Slovaks have climbed to its summit on national pilgrimages.

The Tatras rise suddenly and steeply from flat basins to high mountain altitudes. The varied flora and fauna emphasize their uniqueness. From the basins we climb to a zone of spruce forests

– our Miniature Alps

Ľadový štít
2628 m

Lomnický štít
2632 m

Kežmarský štít
2558 m

Belianske Tatry

Javorový štít
2418 m

Bradavica
2476 m

olský hrebeň

Pät spišských pl.

Téryho
chata

Prostredný
hrebeň

Lomnické
sedlo

Chata pri Zelenom
plese

Ždiar

Zbojnícka
chata

Slavkovský štít
2452 m

Malá studená dolina

Veľká studená dolina

Zamkovského
chata

Skalnaté pleso

Skalnatá
chata

Hotel Encián

Velická dolina

Velické pl.
1663 m

Hrebienok
1263 m

Bilíkova
chata

Kežmarské žľaby

Horský hotel
Sliezsky dom

Tatr. Matliare

Tatr. Lomnica

Tatranská Lesná

Starý Smokovec
1018 m

Horný Smokovec

Tatranské Zruby

Dolný Smokovec

Tatranská Polianka

Poprad
Košice
Bratislava

Nová Lesná

Golden
Eagle

Fox

Brown Bear

Wolf

Marmot

Chamois

from 3,000 to 5,000 feet (800 to 1,500 m) above sea level. Here, spruce and larch dominate the vegetation. In the Belianske Tatras, fir, beech and maple are abundantly represented on limestone soils. Among small shrubs, the bilberry and red bilberry flourish.

If we climb higher, we find that the *Pinus cembra* pine increases on the boundary of the spruce woods. It has a dense egg-shaped crown which provides shelter for many birds; it prevents erosion as well. At a height of 5,000 feet (1,500 m) above sea level, the dense forest thins to scattered groups of trees. Higher, around 5,700 feet (1,800 m) above sea level, a low growth of dwarf pines forms a cover of green.

Above the tree line at 5,700 feet (1,800 m), the climate is too harsh, and only grasses, small shrubs and high mountain flowers can grow here. We call this the level of Alpine grassland. It extends up

to 7,500 feet (2,300 m) above sea level. Here high mountain grasses and meadows dominate, often sprinkled with beautiful multi-colored flowers.
Above this level, there are only disconnected samples of grass, moss and snow.

Many protected flowers grow in the High Tatras. The rarest plants include the Wahlenberg Erysimum, named after a Swedish botanist who worked in the Tatras and published the first book about their flora.

White storks nest in the villages below the Tatras, and on the north side, the rare black stork. Deer are common in the Tatras. Squirrels, smaller carnivores such as the European marten, weasel and fox are numerous near the settlements. The wildcat, lynx, badger, brown bear, woodcock, chamois, marmot and the rare golden eagle occur at higher altitudes.

The picturesque water bodies called tarns (*pleso* in Slovak) form a magnificent contrast to the sharp peaks of the Tatras. There are over a hundred of them, with some in almost every valley. They were dug out by glaciers.

The High Tatras are a magnet for tourists. For the protection of nature and for the safety of visitors, all the tourist paths are marked. Only mountain climbers organized in groups are allowed to go on unmarked routes. Unfortunately, the High Tatras also have their victims. Those who have died there are commemorated in a symbolic cemetery near Poprad Tarn under the peak of Ostrva.

From 1001 Slovak Superlatives

• The High Tatras, our highest, best-known mountain range, is not the most extensive mountain range on Slovak territory, even if we include the Eastern and Belianske Tatras. They have only one-eighth of the area of the Slovak Rudohorie Mountains, the most extensive in Slovakia, with a length of 90 miles (145 km) and a width of 30 to 50 miles (31-47 km).

• Tichá Dolina (Quiet Valley) is the largest mountain valley in Slovakia. It is ten miles (16 km) long and crescent-shaped. Everything in it is associated with quiet. In the north it is divided into Zadná Tichá (Back Quiet) and Temná Tichá (Dark Quiet). Tichý Potok (Quiet Brook) flows through the whole valley, and there is a Tichá gamekeeper's cottage. In contrast to other valleys in the Tatras, it is less visited, therefore quiet.

• Slovak rivers are born in the mountains. And so they leap down the slopes. The fastest of them is the Poprad. It flows from the Mengusovská valley in the Tatras to join the Dunajec in Poland. The difference in height between its ends is 5,140 feet (1,567 m). This is a remarkable drop over a distance of only 107 km.

• The smallest mammal in Slovakia is the lesser shrew. Its length is about 2 inches (4-6 cm) and it weighs less than a quarter ounce (3-5 gm). A restaurant packet of sugar weighs more! The lesser shrew is a very active animal. It climbs on trees, swims well and looks for food both day and night. There is a fine of over 2,000 crowns for killing one. A

lot for such a small animal? Well, no. It is rare and also useful since it eats mostly harmful creatures.

• The master digger of tunnels is the badger, a forest carnivore that weighs up to 45 pounds (20 kg). It creates underground labyrinths with 2-3 levels of tunnels and chambers. The mole is an even more active tunneler. It digs whole palaces with a multitude of passages on different levels. It also makes larger living quarters to provide comfort for mother-moles and their offsprings.

• The biggest fish in Slovakia is the sheat-fish. It has a big head, a wide mouth with 6 whiskers around it, small eyes, a plump body and varied coloring. The largest catch recorded in Slovakia was in 1965 on the River Bodrog. It measured 8´8" (265 cm) and weighed 280 pounds (128 kg).

• The deadliest tree is the yew. It excels especially in the hardness of its wood and remarkable resistance to weather, but it has another notorious property. It is the most poisonous tree, its leaves in particular. If an animal eats only a small amount it dies. Surprisingly, goats are not harmed.

• The most tilted tower - with a tilt of 6.0 inches (151 cm) - stands at Ivánka near Nitra. It is surpassed by the world record-holder in Pisa, which leans by 20.4 inches (518 cm).

*From the book
by L. Švihran,*
1000+1 Slovak Superlatives

THE LEGENDARY JÁNOŠÍK

Jánošík with his band of outlaws - Slovak folk painting on glass from the first half of the 19th century

Fair little Jánošík,
Curly-haired child,
If you hadn't stolen,
They wouldn't have caught you...

Juro Jánošík was a folk hero who robbed the rich and gave to the poor. He was born at Terchová in 1688. When Jánošík's father was almost beaten to death by a bailiff because he was sick and could not go to work for his lord, Jánošík gave up his studies, went to the mountains and later became chief of a band of outlaws. The people loved him, but in the end Jánošík was hung for his deeds. But he continued to live on – the Jánošík tradition was born.

Jánošík and his outlaws appear in folk art – songs, poems, stories, legends, paintings on glass and in wood carvings. In the 19th century, literature continued the folk tradition, and produced further works of art. The first film about Jánošík was made in 1921. A version with sound appeared in 1936. The composer Ján Cikker is author of a national opera bearing the name of Juro Jánošík.

Stories about Jánošík's adventures and mischievous deeds are still a fruitful theme. Here are some stories which are still alive today.

Turning over a Stone

Jánošík could turn over really enormous stones. There was a stone in our parish, big enough for a man to sleep on. Jánošík wrote on it:

"Whoever turns this stone over will not go unrewarded!"

And so men went there with oxen and dug under the stone so that they could turn it over. But when they had turned it over, they found written on the other side:

"Thank you very much. I've been lying on this side for long enough."

He made jokes like that.

Playing at Being Outlaws

When Jánošík was already a famous outlaw, a certain lord arranged a banquet at his mansion and an entertainment for his guests. He ordered some of his retainers to dress like Jánošík's men and come to entertain the guests. Jánošík learned of this. He and his men also came to the mansion in secret, tied up the pretend outlaws, and went into the banqueting hall themselves. First they danced some outlaw dances, then they asked the magnates for jewels. The guests were enraptured by the dance, and in the belief that the jewels would

be returned to them, they even competed to give the most. But this was not enough for Jánošík's men, and they began to tear off jewels which the guests did not want to give. The guests began to get irritated by such effrontery, since it was only supposed to be a game. Then they began to recognize Jánošík's men. By the time that the guests had recovered from their dismay and freed the tied-up retainers, Jánošík's men had long since reached safety.

The Robbed Inn-keeper

When Jánošík was robbing with his comrades, he once came to a certain inn, where there was music and dancing. The inn belonged to a young inn-keeper, a very rich widow. She liked Jánošík and began to talk with him. His comrades remained outside. It was evening. Jánošík had given them secret orders, saying that since he wouldn't be able to talk to them, the should perform what he sang accompanying the music. First he sang:

Good evening
Dear inn-keeper,
I heard long ago
That you are a widow,
And a young widow
And very rich,
That you have much silver
And even more gold.

Over good wine, Jánošík made merry and started to dance with

the inn-keeper. She was charmed by his handsome appearance and thought of nothing but how to win Jánošík as her husband. She got careless and showed Jánošík the chest in the storeroom, where she kept her gold ducats. When the inn-keeper went away, Jánošík sang:

My comrades
Go to the storeroom,
Grease a hand-saw with tallow
And cut open the chest.

His comrades understood, went to the storeroom and took whatever they liked. Others kept watch for them. But the inn-keeper in the dance was not worried about anything. Jánošík knew that his comrades were not idle. When he thought that they were ready, he sang:

My comrades,
Go to the stable,
Saddle the horses
And get mounted.
Leave the grey one for me.

His comrades understood. They also took the inn-keeper's horses. At an appropriate moment, Jánošík left the inn, got on the grey mare and followed his comrades, who were already far away.

From the book: Witty Stories and Great Tricks and Jokes – Humor and Satire in Slovak Folk Tales. *Compiled by Viera Gašparíková*

Skillful Hands and Fantasy

The products of the busy hands of our ancestors – superb embroideries, paintings, pottery, woodwork, leather, and metal products and tools – made life easier, and bringing beauty into everyday life. Traditional Slovak artistic objects are still produced today to please the eye and for the practical purposes they have had for centuries.

Wirework

Wirework originated in the Váh Valley and Kysuce regions. It was stimulated by poverty and the search for new ways of making a living. Poor wireworkers used wire to repair broken pottery plates, bowls and jars so that they were strengthened with a wire network.

They also made birdcages, clothes-hangers, mousetraps and many other useful things from wire. Many wireworkers went abroad. There, the richer ones established famous wireworking workshops. The poorer ones sold their wire products as peddlers. Some wireworkers also achieved artistic success. In the 20th century, wireworking as a craft disappeared; but the artistic feeling of the wireworkers can still be seen, for example, in the permanent exhibition of wirework art in Budatín Castle.

Oil Production

Oil production is one of the traditional Slovak crafts. Production and trade in oil became very wide-

spread in the 18th and early 19th centuries; but the history of oil production goes further back into the past. The oldest oils include dwarf pine, juniper, cumin and olive oil, and oil from pine cones. They were based on vegetable ethers obtained by distillation or pressing from various cones, seeds and twigs. The growth of oil production was stimulated by poor health care and the small number of pharmacies. Slovak oil makers sold their products to almost the whole of Europe. Preparations and oils were offered in little bottles and jars, and were frequently trade-marked with a seal. Servants carried them in a special box.

Rafting

In the past, our ancestors transported tree trunks in water. First they gradually collected the trunks on the bank of a river and fastened them together to make a raft. Then they attached a rudder to it, brought food, some pots and other necessities, and set off on their journey.

They transported the timber or raft to where it was needed. They also transported cargoes such as salt or ore, and passengers – soldiers – on rafts.

Today rafting occurs only on the Dunajec as a tourist attraction. Rafting is first mentioned in writing in an endowment document of St. Benedict Abbey in 1075. Up to the 16th century, we know little about rafting. We assume that it developed in the 13th to 14th centuries during the settlement of the mountain regions. Even in the last century, timber for building and fuel was floated from the upper Hron to Esztergom and Budapest. The importance of rafting as a means of transport declined with the construction of railways and dams on the rivers, which made rafting impossible at some sections.

Wood is the oldest material from which tools were made. In Slovakia there was and still is plenty of wood. It became a favorite material for its good properties. They made almost everything from it – means of transport, household implements, tools for shepherds, weavers, and carpenters, weapons and moulds for cooking.

Leatherwork

Prehistoric man was a hunter, and leather was already a basic material for the production of clothes and shoes thousands of years ago. Leather belts were made by the skilled hands of sad-dlers. In the 18th century, they began to make small metal ornaments for horse harness and belts.

Wide man's belt with four buckles, from Partizánska Lupča

Copperwork

The craft of the coppersmith originated in the 15th and 16th centuries. The craftsmen used easily workable copper and brass plate. By cold hammering they made kettles, jugs, bottles, candlesticks and other household objects. They tin-plated the inside of vessels for food or drink so that poisonous verdigris would not contaminate the food or drink. With the development of industrial production, coppersmithing disappeared.

Copper kettle from the 18th century, Trnava, domestic work

Pottery

Pottery originated in prehistoric times. Originally pots were made by women. The Celts introduced the potter's wheel to Slovakia. Later the Slavs continued to use manual potter's wheels and in the time of Great Moravia pottery had already reached a high level of craftsmanship. Slovak ceramics, which arose from domestic pottery, take pride in their wealth of color, shape and design. In the 18th century, Slovak ceramics developed further. Apart from functional items, figurines were also made. Pottery from Modra, Pukanec, Pozdišovce, Levice, Holíč, Bardejov and other towns and areas of Slovakia is still very popular. Haban pottery forms a distinct group. The Habans were descendants of German Anabaptists, settled in western Slovakia. Their rounded jugs have short necks and special designs.

Leather bag with buckle and brass ornaments

Haban pottery

38

Honey-Cake Production

Honey-cake production is known in Slovakia from the 14th century. In the 16th century, it separated from the craft of baking; and at the beginning of the 17th century, the first honey-cake maker's guild in the Kingdom of Hungary was established in Bratislava. Honey-cake makers also devoted themselves to the production of wax objects, making candles, torches and other things apart from honey-cakes. In the 17th century, honey-cake makers used wooden moulds, which they made from pear wood, or had them made by wood-carvers. The design of the moulds was quite varied; and each crafts-man strove to create the most beautiful, in the shape of hearts, horses, hussars, little houses or babies. The surface of honey-cakes was later elabo-rately decorated.

Basket-Making

Basket-making already flourished in the 10th century. The masters of the craft used various tech-niques – tying, weaving, pulling and plaiting techniques. Most fre-quently they used strips of wood and twigs from oak, hazel and maple trees. They made door-mats, dolls, sandals and bags from corn husks. These products are still popular today. Basket-mak-ing gradually declined, but cen-ters for basket-making still exist.

Major ar-tists such as the writer Ján Botto and the painter Mar-tin Benka concerned them-selves with the theme of rafting.

39

Wooden Treasures

Water mill
at Jahodná

Slovaks were born to work with wood. Wood accompanied them from the cradle, was the basic building material of houses, churches, belfries and agricultural buildings (stables, hay-barns, stores, shepherds' huts). The number of preserved wooden buildings in Slovakia is staggering. Every cottage, church or belfry testifies to the high level of culture of our ancestors, their inborn feel for architecture and master craftsmanship, as well as to the close connection of man with nature and natural materials.

Stove in a Detva living room

Cottage at Čičmany

Many buildings are not only useful, but also beautiful because of the harmony between their design and their surroundings.

The water mill at Jahodná on the Little Danube is a surviving monument of the ancient builder's and miller's crafts. In fact the oldest finds of millstones date from the Celtic period. Water mills were common, especially on the rivers Váh and Danube. However, the character of the country does not favor wind mills, which were rare in Slovakia.

Čičmany is a remarkable village, first mentioned in a document from 1272. Traditional folk architecture is preserved in the village. The houses are built of logs with shingle roofs, and have one or two stories. They have store rooms accessible through verandas. The houses are decorated with beautiful white patterns, which are concentrated just below the roof.

This wooden church at Mirol'a, a tiny village in East Slovakia, is one of Slovakia's most beautiful wooden treasures

The hands of unknown folk carpenters built this wooden belfry in Zemplín at the beginning of the 19th century.

This farm house in Šaľa is built of unbaked brick clay, and covered with a thatched roof. The house has excellent heat insulation properties. Šaľa, first mentioned in 1002, is one of the oldest communities in Slovakia.

The houses of Heľpa are built of logs and have cellars. They have verandas on their entrance sides. At Heľpa, they made wooden tools for shepherds. Wood carving and weaving also flourished here. They hold a folklore festival at Heľpa every year.

The kitchen and living room were arranged simply, but very practically. Both rooms were dominated by a stove which heated them as well. The household equipment was very simple, and made of clay, wood and metal. The oldest pieces of furniture originate from the Middle Ages. A chest made from a single section of a tree was the most treasured. Later (in the 14th to 15th centuries), they began to make chests with lids. The front walls of the chest were painted. From the 17th century, cupboards with two doors began to replace chests. The furniture reflected the position of the family.

Wooden folk architecture at Heľpa

Jaseno - peasant living room

41

The Charm of Slovak Embroidery

Nobody in the whole world has such a rich and varied range of folk costume in such a small area as Slovaks is. The folk costumes — evidence of a rich cultural history — constantly fascinate artists, photographers and ethnographers. Today it is rare to see people wearing folk costumes in their everyday lives; but on ceremonial occasions this wealth shines in its full glory and beauty. When welcoming important guests with bread and salt, at folklore celebrations, or at church services like weddings and funerals, at church services, the folk costumes come out of their chests, and the young take pride in the skill of their grandmothers.

The male folk costume of Detva is very original. The shirt reaches to the middle of the chest, and the trousers are wide. Both parts of the costume are made from white home made linen. The sleeves are exactly as wide as the length of the shirt. Even today it is said that the people of Detva have bare navels. The trousers were held up by a belt decorated with ornamental buckles. A hat with decorative leather thongs covered long hair braided into four plaits. With the embroidered costume, they carried a shepherd's hatchet.

Two Goral villages in Northern Orava — Hladovka and Suchá Hora — have a very remarkable costume. The cloth trousers have wide ornamental borders on the side seams with black woolen laces. A fur coat of brown lamb skin, typical of the Goral costume, is decorated with colored embroidery. The hat is decorated with a feather from a hawk, eagle or buzzard. The ceremonial costume from Bošáca in West Slovakia is very special. It excels in the magnificence of its fine embroidery, the most finest in the whole of Slovakia. The colored embroidery on the apron has the character of a detailed mosaic. High black boots complete the ceremonial costume.

Male costume from
Detva

Ceremonial costumes
from Bošáca

Male costume from
Hladovka and Suchá
Hora

*Embroidery from Parchovany
in the district of Michalovce*

The men´s and women´s costumes from Trenčianska Teplá, in which the colors red, yellow, black and white dominated, were richly decorated. The black waistcoat has rich embroidery. A flower was embroidered in the center of the back. Sometimes the date was added.

The folk costumes are the message of past generations. We must value and protect this treasure so that those who come after us can also enjoy the beauty we have inherited.

The costumes are documents of the past existence of the nation, its fantasies and artistic feelings. They speak eloquently of the life of people in the areas from which they come, and about the aesthetic feelings of the nation. They made the costumes from natural materials, especially hemp, flax and skins. In the 19th century, they added rich embellishments with colored threads to the previously modest embroidery. The use of industrially - produced materials, such as cotton, satin, blue printed cloth and metal also spread.

At folklore festivals and in museums, the magnificent world of richly embroidered ruffles, skirts, hats and aprons continue to fascinate Slovak and foreign visitors, both experts and the general public.

One of the methods of embroidery is called embroidery with a curved needle. This embroidery comes from a Detva costume. The ornament is mostly geometric and has a yellow base supplemented by red and later blue. Embroidery with a curved needle was first practiced at the beginning of the 20th century.

Men´s and women´s costumes from Trenčianska Teplá   *Costumes from Liptovské Sliače*

This important Christian feast, associated with the coming of spring, is also reflected in folk customs and traditions.

Our ancestors welcomed the coming of spring by drowning Morena (old Slavonic goddess of night, winter and death). Girls carried a straw figure of Morena from the village to the stream two weeks before Easter on "Death Sunday."

In Slovakia, they carried a little tree with ribbons and egg shells hanging from it through the villages, on Palm Sunday, the sunday before Easter. The Church introduced this feast in the 7th century.

EASTER

During the Easter festival, the girls and boys wore richly decorated costumes. The custom of decorating homes at Easter with branches of blossoming willow (catkins) is still preserved today. The catkins symbolize new life. The rabbit, an animal noted for its fecundity, is also a symbol of Easter.

The last days before Easter

On **Maundy Thursday**, young nettles and dandelions were cooked and eaten. The shepherds drove out evil spirits by blowing trumpets.

Good Friday was the greatest day of fasting in the year. On this day the "earth could not be disturbed," and people did not work in the fields.

On **Holy Saturday** – after 40 long days of fasting came the evening celebration of the Resurrection of Christ. People had a rich dinner, resembling that of Christmas Eve.

Easter Sunday – one of the most beautiful Christian feast-days.

Easter Monday – Amid the general rejoicing, the boys would whip the girls and drench them with water. In some regions, young men still weave whips from willow twigs, and use them to whip the single girls and the married women. The girls tied colored ribbons to the whips. In spite of the spring cold, the boys were not sparing with the water, and all the girls got soaking wet.

– The Spring Festival

Easter was preceded by the 40-day fast of Lent, and before this came Shrovetide or Carnival (*Fašiangy* in Slovak), a happy time full of song, entertainment and merrymaking.

Shrovetide, Whitsuntide, Easter is coming;
Who has no fur coat will be cold,
I have none, I have none,
So I am shivering.
Give me some bacon,
So I'll have something to eat.

A folk song from Podkonice

Kraslice are painted or otherwise decorated eggs, which girls made to reward the boys who whipped them. They dipped or boiled eggs in water with winter corn, tree-bark, onion peels and other things. They often decorated them with bees' wax. In Spiš they scratched designs onto the colored egg with a knife. In West Slovakia, they stuck barley straw colored onto the eggs, or decorated them with wire. Around Lučenec, they covered them with metal.

A wooden well is difficult to find today, but in the past there was one in every prosperous courtyard. By turning the wheel, a wooden bucket on a chain was lowered into the well. It was heavy and sank into the water, which was drawn into it. Then by turning the wheel and winding up the chain, the bucket came up full. And then the water went straight onto the shouting girls.

CHRISTMAS – The Most

A festival of peace, love, and abundance, rich in tradition and woven around with mystery. The Slovaks' pagan ancestors celebrated the Winter Solstice, since the old sun departed then and a new one was born. Christianity added to this festival a deeper meaning expressed by the biblical message of the love of God for all people of good will. Thus in Slovakia Christianity took over many pagan customs and gave them a humane New Testament message.

Christians celebrate Christmas as the day of the birth of Jesus at Bethlehem. Families prepared for it for weeks in advance. They cleaned the home, baked cakes, made decorations for the tree. The period of preparation for Christmas is called Advent.

Beautiful ancient customs were observed, especially on the feasts of St. Nicholas (December 6th) and St. Lucy (December 13th).

Originally, when there was little space in cottages, the Christmas tree was hung from a wooden beam, and they decorated it with little apples, nuts and straw figures. Under the tree was placed the crib (*Betlehem* in Slovak), the scene of the birth of Jesus, made from corn husks or carved wood, which brought the mystery of the birth of Jesus into the home.

On Christmas Eve, the family had dinner after fasting all day. Most dinner tables enjoyed:

- **a lighted candle** – its light helping the Wise Men to find their way to the crib
- **wafers** – symbolizing the communion of all Christians
- **honey, nuts, little apples** – gifts of nature securing health
- **garlic and onion** – protection from every evil
- **fish scales** – supposed to bring the family money and happiness
- **a piece of bread and glass of water** – everyday necessities of life.

Beautiful Festival of the Year

The little apples had a symbolic character. After dinner the father cut one up. If it was good, a peaceful year awaited the family. Everyone took a piece of the apple, so that in the following year they would always find a safe way home.

The Christmas Eve dinner was bountiful. Its bounty was reflected in the number of foods. All the fruits or produce of the soil they had grown during the year were brought to the table in turn. They had lentil or cabbage soup, baked pasta balls with poppy seed, cakes and other local foods. Later they included fish in the Christmas Eve dinner. Today this is the most frequent Christmas Eve food.

One of the most beautiful Christmas carols runs:

Christ the Lord is born today,
Let us rejoice.
From the rose a flower bloomed,
Let us be glad.
From a life immaculate,
From a royal family,
Christ the Lord
is born today.

Pokoj ľuďom dobrej vôle

Food would also be saved for carol-singers and people bringing their Christmas greetings. Peasants also took a little of each food and gave it to the domestic animals.

Christmas Eve was enlivened by people coming to sing carols and wish health and happiness.

In the festive atmosphere, the eyes of the children shone in the expectation of presents and the decorated tree. In time, mistletoe, which grows on the tops of trees, also became part of our decorations.

Slovak Coins and Banknotes

Celtic coins struck in Bratislava

Celtic silver coin with the inscription BIATEC, found in Bratislava (obverse and reverse)

In ancient times people traded by exchanging goods. The prehistoric hunter exchanged skins and meat for forest products or a building. This natural trade was inconvenient and cumbersome. Everything changed when the ancient Phoenicians invented money.

In the 4th century B.C., the Celts controlled a large part of Western and Central Europe, including the Carpathian basin. A Celtic mint was established in Bratislava in the 1st century before Christ. It stood where the Pálffy Palace on Panská Street stands today. The Bratislava mint reached the pinnacle of Celtic coin production.

Today money is used for trade. It is also an expression of the maturity of the nation that issues it. Therefore national heroes, rulers, and symbols are depicted on money.

The basic monetary unit in Slovakia is the Slovak crown, or koruna, abbreviated to Sk. The crown is made up of 100 haliers. New coins and banknotes have been used in Slovakia since 1993.

Smaller coins worth 10, 20 and 50 haliers, and larger coins worth 1, 2, 5 and 10 crowns are in circulation. For larger amounts, there are banknotes of 20, 50, 100, 200, 500, 1000 and 5000 crowns.

Money also expresses the value of the work needed to earn it, and we should treat it with respect. It is necessary to handle it carefully. It should be folded only in unavoidable cases; it may not be damaged, defaced or shrunk. Every citizen shows his level of maturity by his treatment of money.

The obverse sides of the coins are the same. They show the state emblem of the Slovak Republic, the inscription "Slovenská Republika" and the year of issue. The reverse sides document life in Slovakia in various historical periods.

- on the 10 halier coin, a 19th century wooden belfry from Zemplín is depicted,
- on the 20 halier coin, the peak of Kriváň in the Tatras, a symbol of Slovakia,
- on the 50 halier coin, part of the Devín Castle,
- on the 1 crown coin is a wooden Gothic statue of the Madonna and Child, made around 1500, from Kremnica,
- on the 2 crown coin is a sitting Venus, or the Great Mother from the 4th millennium before Christ, found at Nitriansky Hrádok (today part of Šurany),
- on the 5 crown is the design of a Celtic coin with the inscription BIATEC from the 1st century before Christ (see the Celtic coin at left),
- on the 10 crown coin is a cast bronze cross from the second half of the 9th to the 10th century. It is an archaeological find from Veľká Mača in the district of Galanta.

Coin of King Stephen I struck in the Bratislava Castle. On the reverse is the Latin inscription — Breslava Civitas — The City of Breslav."

100 Sk - on the front, the Madonna by Master Pavol of Levoča, on the back, architectural elements of Levoča

200 Sk - on the front, Anton Bernolák, on the back, a design representing the churches of Trnava

20 Sk - on the front is Pribina and on the back, Nitra Castle and objects recalling his principality

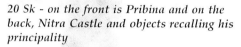

500 Sk - on the front, Ľudovít Štúr, on the back, Bratislava Castle and the oldest map of Bratislava, from the 15th century

50 Sk - on the front Saints Cyril and Methodius, on the back, examples of Glagolithic letters and the little church at Dražovce

1000 Sk - on the front, portrait of Andrej Hlinka, on the back, designs connected with the places where he worked

5000 Sk - on the front, portrait of Milan Rastislav Štefánik, on the back, his grave monument on Bradlo, as well as designs connected with his scientific activity

Milestones on Slovakia's Road to Independence

The first independent state of the Slavonic tribes inhabiting the Danube basin was Samo's Empire (623-658).

From the beginning of the 9th century, the significant Slavonic principalities of Nitra, Moravia and Pannonia arose in the territory of modern Slovakia, Moravia and Hungary. Great Moravia originated after 833 from the union of the principalities of Nitra and Moravia. Its rulers were Mojmír I (833-846), Rastislav (846-870), Slavomír (870-871), Svätopluk I (871-894) and Mojmír II (894-907). The sons of Svätopluk, Mojmír II and Svätopluk II, quarreled over their shares of power in Great Moravia, and warlike tribes of old Hungarian or Magyar raiders took advantage of it. After the Magyars won a battle near Bratislava in 907, the power of Great Moravia was finally broken. As a result of their quarrels, the Slovaks lost their independence for more than a thousand years. The fall of Great Moravia was the result of the fragmentation of the princely power into smaller territorial units. The invasion of the Magyars did not encounter united resistance. Nevertheless the tradition and spirit of Great Moravia survived into the Middle Ages, and has been revived again in the modern history of the Slovaks.

Rapid and unexpected attacks on the inhabitants of the Danube basin by the nomadic Magyar tribes began in 896. By the time of their defeat in 955, the Magyar tribes had changed from steppe pastoralism to cattle breeding and agriculture. The most important leader of the Magyar tribes was Géza from the Árpád family. Before his death in 997, he and his son Vajka accepted baptism and both took the Christian name Stephen.

The younger Stephen, founder of the Árpád dynasty, became the first King of a new European feudal state, Hungary. He took over much of the economic development, territorial administration, culture and art of Great Moravia, and ruled wisely and justly from 1000 to 1038. He accepted the Christianity of the Western, or Latin rite. The important monarchs of the Árpád dynasty included Ladislav I (1077- 1095) and Béla IV (1235-1270). Both strengthened the royal power and the internal affairs of the Kingdom of Hungary.

The granting of the Golden Bull of King Andrew II in 1222 was a turning point in the history of Hungary. It gave greater power to the nobility, who could administer the territory entrusted to them without the intervention of the King.

According to the constitution of the old Kingdom of Hungary, all offices and titles were approved by parliament. This continued until 1848.

In 1458, the Hungarian parliament elected a new King, Matthias Corvinus, who introduced many reforms to support the towns and the lesser nobility. He built up a strong army, which was able to resist the growing Turkish threat. The less able successors of Matthias Corvinus could not resist the growing Turkish pressure. In 1526, the Turks completely crushed the Hungarian army at the Battle of Mohács.

The succession of the Emperor Ferdinand I to the throne of Hungary in 1526 began the rule of the HaBsburg dynasty in Hungary. Ferdinand I, who also ruled Austria and Bohemia, laid the foundations of a multinational state.

The most important monarch of the 18th century was Maria Theresa, who ruled from 1740 to 1780. She introduced many important reforms. According to her educational reforms, all young people, even in the villages, had to receive primary education. Even more extensive reforms were introduced by her son, Joseph II (1780-1790). The most important were the abolition of serfdom in his own domains, and the Edict of Toleration, which abolished discrimination against the non-Catholic inhabitants of the Empire.

The replacement of Latin by German as the official language of the Kingdom of Hungary stimulated the students of theology centered around Anton Bernolák to develop Slovak into a literary language suitable for publishing. In 1792, a national cultural society, called the Slovak Learned Guild, was established.

The Hungarian pressure drew the Slovak Catholics and Protestants closer to each other. Already before the revolution, in 1844, the Tatrín society was formed, with the aim of achieving national unity of the Slovaks. In 1845, Ľudovít Štúr began to publish the *Slovak National Newspaper* with its supplement, *The Tatran Eagle*, which had great influence on forming the national consciousness of the Slovaks.

In 1847, Štúr became a member of the Hungarian Parliament in Bratislava, with demands to abolish serfdom, guarantee the political rights of the people, abolish the privileges of the nobility, secure education of the people, and use Slovak in the state administration and in church services. Štúr had to make his memorable speech in Hungarian.

The ideals of the French Revolution of 1789 — Liberty, Equality, Fraternity — penetrated the whole of Europe and provoked uprisings in most states. On March 13, 1848 rioting broke out in Vienna, and two days later the insurrection spread to Pest. The Hungarian Parliament abolished the privileges of the nobility and declared the independence of Hungary from the Vienna government. Next arose the problem of the relations between the Magyars (Hungarians) and the non-Magyar majority of the population of the Kingdom of Hungary. The middle nobility, led by Lajos Kossuth, unleashed a fanatical Magyar campaign in all areas of public life, with the slogan "One homeland, one language, one nation."

The representatives of the Slovak national movement included Štúr, Hurban, Hodža, Daxner and Francisci. In May 1848, they worked out the *Demands of the Slovak Nation*, which contained the national and social demands of the Slovak movement. The Budapest government responded to this national program, proclaimed in Liptovský Svätý Mikuláš, by ordering the arrest of Štúr, Hurban and Hodža. The other non-Magyar peoples living in the Kingdom of Hungary (Romanians, Serbs and Croats) also came up with similar demands.

In September 1848, Štúr, together with Hurban and Hodža, began to prepare Slovak volunteers for an armed uprising. It was headed by the Slovak National Council, formed at Myjava. The first armed uprising of Slovaks seeking their independence lasted only a few days; and although the Czechs, Moravians and Croats sympathized with it, it was unsuccessful.

After the defeat of Austria by Prussia in 1867, the Vienna court had to hand over all power in the Kingdom of Hungary to the Magyars. A new state was formed, Austria-Hungary, which was a great success for the Magyars (Hungarians), but a great disappointment for the Czechs and Slovaks, who longed to gain autonomy.

In 1875, Koloman Tisza, who proclaimed that he recognized no Slovak nation, became prime minister of Hungary. He began a great campaign against the Slovaks. In the school year 1887- 1888, about 500 Slovak children were removed from Slovakia and placed with Magyar families in the southern region. About 300 of them later returned home after terrible hardship and mostly on foot. Slovak schools and societies were closed; the leading figures of the national movement were imprisoned. Appónyi, the minister of education from 1906 to 1910, made the greatest effort to Magyarize Slovak schools.

In 1896, the Society of Czechoslovak Unity was founded in Prague, with the aim of strengthening relations between the Czechs and the Slovaks.

The disputes between the states of the Triple Alliance (Germany, Austria-Hungary and Italy) and the Triple Entente (Great Britain, France and Russia) led to the First World War. Many oppressed nations used the war as a struggle for national liberation.

In 1916, the Czechoslovak National Council was formed in Paris as the supreme organ of the struggle abroad. Until the end of the war it was led by Tomáš Garrigue Masaryk, Milan Rastislav Štefánik and Edvard Beneš.

On October 28, 1918, the Czechoslovak National Committee in Prague proclaimed the Czechoslovak Republic. Masaryk became its first president.

On October 30, 1918, at Turčiansky Svätý Martin, the Slovaks, through their Slovak National Council, issued the Martin Declaration, identifying themselves with the common state of the Czechs and Slovaks, in which the two nations would live together as equals. The creation of a democratic republic meant great progress for the Slovaks, especially in comparison with the feudal situation in the old Kingdom of Hungary.

Slovakia lagged behind the Czech lands not only in industry, but also in agricultural production. Even from the beginning of the common state, many Slovaks demanded that Prague grant Slovakia autonomy. According to the Pittsburgh Agreement, signed on May 31, 1918 by representatives of Czech and Slovak organizations in the U. S. during the visit of Masaryk, these demands were to be satisfied in the new republic. The autonomist movement was led by Andrej Hlinka.

However, the Prague politicians insisted on the existence of a "Czechoslovak nation" which included the Slovaks. This idea was especially supported by the second Czechoslovak president Edvard Beneš.

Slovakia, with the help of the victorious Western powers, defeated an invasion by the Hungarian army (1918-1919), which aimed to reunite Slovakia with Hungary. In June 1919, a Slovak Soviet Republic was even proclaimed at Prešov. Its aim was the union of Slovakia with Hungary, and it was under the influence of the Hungarian Soviet Republic. It lasted only a few days.

On June 4, 1920, a treaty was signed at Trianon in France. By it, the international community confirmed the origin of the successor states after the break-up of the old Kingdom of Hungary, the frontiers between them, and the duties of the newly formed Hungarian state towards them.

The Great Depression of 1929 — 1933 had a severe effect on Slovakia too, which solved its deteriotating social situation by large-scale emigration.

At the end of September 1938, a conference of the four great powers — France, Great Britain, Italy and Germany — was held in Munich. Hitler demanded the cession of the Czech frontier regions, where more than three and a half million Germans lived, to the Nazi Germany. Czechoslovakia could not fight the strong German army without foreign help, so it was forced to accept Hitler's ultimatum. President Beneš resigned on October 4, 1938 and went into exile in Great Britain.

Two days after the resignation of Beneš, by the Žilina Agreement the majority of the Slovak political parties accepted a proposed constitutional amendment on the autonomy of Slovakia. The Prague government accepted the autonomy of Slovakia and renamed the state Czecho-Slovakia.

In November 1938, the foreign ministers of Germany and Italy signed a decision, the Vienna Arbitration, according to which Czecho-slovakia had to give up a significant part of Slovakia and Sub-Carpathian Ruthenia to the Hungary, and border territory of Tešín to Poland.

Hitler regarded the territories of Bohemia and Moravia as part of the medieval German Empire, and he wanted to annex them to his new Germany. Using as his pretext the disputes between the Prague government and the autonomous government of Slovakia on March 13, 1939, he invited Jozef Tiso, prime minister of Slovakia, to Berlin and gave him two choices: either proclaim an independent state, or Slovakia would be divided between Germany, Poland and Hungary.

On March 14, 1939, a meeting of parliament was called in Bratislava, and declared Slovakia independent. Jozef Tiso became the first President of the Slovak Republic. Although the Slovak Republic ex-

isted as a protectorate of the German Reich, the great majority of states recognized it and established diplomatic relations with it.

On September 1, 1939, the German army invaded Poland without the declaration of war. This marked the beginning of the Second World War. But Hitler's initially successful conquest of Europe collapsed after five years.

In August 1944, the Red Army began its victorious advance into South-Eastern and Central Europe, gradually liberating the occupied countries. On June 29, 1944, the Slovak National Uprising began. Apart from Slovak partisans, members of 26 nations and nationalities in the Red Army participated in it. Thus the Slovak nation proved its opposition to fascism and interest in a democratic future. On May 8, 1945, Germany signed an unconditional surrender. We celebrate this day as the end of the war in Europe.

On April 4, 1945, a Popular Front government was formed in the liberated part of Czechoslovakia, and on April 5 it proclaimed the Košice Manifesto. Representatives of the Slovak parties demanded an equal position for the two nations in a Czecho-Slovak Republic. However, the unequal relationship between the Czechs and Slovaks continued and lasted until 1968.

The totalitarian system, installed in Czechoslovakia after the February coup d'etat of 1948, collapsed in the crisis of 1968, which was provoked by the innovations of Alexander Dubček. Since Prague was the capital of the republic, it led the struggle for reform of the political and social system known as the "Prague Spring." In August 1968, on the basis of Slovak demands, a document about a federal reorganization of Czecho-Slovakia was signed in the Bratislava Castle. However this was only a sym-

bolic gesture, since most constitutional power still remained in Prague.

The Soviet leader Leonid Brezhnev and the leaders of the other states of the Warsaw Pact (East Germany, Poland, Bulgaria and Hungary) saw Dubček and his supporters as a threat to their position, so on August 21, 1968, they invaded Czechoslovakia and occupied it. Dubček and his supporters were removed from public life, and the period of "normalization" began.

In Spring 1988, Slovak Christians demonstrated in Bratislava against the brutality of the political and state system in Slovakia. The demonstration was broken up, but the final phase of the collapse of totalitarianism began here.

On November 17, 1989, a student demonstration in Prague marked the beginning of the "Velvet Revolution."

However, even the fall of the totalitarian system did not bring Slovakia the power to decide things for itself. Prague remained the political and economic center, and Slovak interests did not find the adequate response. This led to the break up of the Czecho-Slovak Federation, and the origin of an independent Slovakia.

On July 17, 1992, the Slovak National Council declar ed sovereignty, and on September 1, 1992, approved the Constitution of the Slovak Republic.

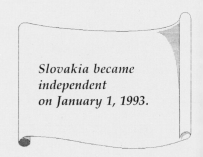

Slovakia became independent on January 1, 1993.

SLOVAKIA TODAY

Not only has Slovakia a rich past, but also an exciting present. It is young, but with old traditions. The hard work, creativity and thought of the people of Slovakia have created a vibrant, progressive country. Slovakia has skillful people, good engineering and chemical industries, and agriculture all comparable in quality to those of any other nation.

The greatest treasure of Slovakia is its people. The Slovaks are peace-loving, modest and patriotic. They know how to defend their own, and the slogan, "We don't need foreigners, we'll defend ourselves," is a good summary of this characteristic feature of the nation.

The greatest treasure of a nation is its education. Knowledge not only enriches, it also makes people better. Every year, 680,000 pupils attend grammar schools. Over 300,000 students study at secondary schools and almost 70,000 students attend colleges or universities.

Tradition is also part of the wealth of the nation. The Slovaks, as an ancient people with unique folklore, as well as longlasting and beautiful folk customs and songs, know very well what has been entrusted to them. They preserve their traditions, develop them, and constantly present them at home and abroad in renewed beauty, as in the case of the song "Dance, dance, whirl around." Slovakia´s unspoiled countryside is beautiful too—fertile plains in the south, the sky-touching Tatras in the north to please the eyes of both Slovaks and visitors from abroad.

Slovak industry cannot be faulted. The sheet steel and other products from the East Slovakia Ironworks at Košice are known throughout the world. Railway cars from Poprad run on French and German tracks. Washing machines from Poprad, televisions from Nižná in Orava, ships from Komárno, chemical products from all over Slovakia, and glass from Lednické Rovne or Utekáč

are known around the world. Finally, Slovak wine, beer, meat and dairy products all show how bountiful a table Slovakia spreads for itself and for its friends worldwide.

The natural beauty of Slovakia is appreciated by everybody who has visited the High or Low Tatras. Slovenský Raj (the Slovak Paradise) is also magnificent. Caverns with their stalactites, such as Demänová and Driny, the Dobšiná Ice Cavern and the Ochtince Aragonite Cavern are also popular. The Herľany geyser and the untamed Dunajec River are also unique features. Among wild life, the rare golden eagle and the bustard, Europe's largest bird, are especially interesting. Forests full of animals, including bears, and the European bison at Topoľčianky, are also attractions. Tourists appreciate Slovak cuisine, with dishes such as "bryndzové halušky" (potato dumplings with sheep cheese) and "pirohy" (boiled stuffed dumplings), roast goose with "lokše" (crisp potato pancakes), "haruľa" (fried potato pancake) or Gemer meat balls.

As a foreign tourist once said, Slovakia is a concentration of all types of natural beauty, and for perfection only the sea is missing. Well, Slovak engineers and workers are doing their best to create man-made lakes instead. Among the largest are Liptovská Mara, Oravská Priehrada, Zemplínska Šírava, and, most recently, the lake of Gabčíkovo. Czechoslovakia and Hungary began to build it in 1977, and the Slovaks have completed their part; now in operation are the Gabčíkovo hydro-electric power station and two locks for ships. These lift ships going towards Bratislava and lower those going towards Komárno, since there is a difference of 75 feet (23m) in the level of the river at the Gabčíkovo Dam. Thanks to this work, a large lake has been formed, which will be used for recreation; and the Danubian river-side forests have been restored.

What is Slovakia today? Like a girl who is growing in beauty, like a youth who is coming of age, like wine maturing in the cellars of working people, like the sun rising over the Tatras.

Milan Rúfus

Prayer for Slovakia

I know a nest, I like it much.
In it, as in God's nest
Are many fathers, many mothers
And many, many children.

The Creator made this nest,
And also decided for whom:
Whom he would invite to live there
In a human home,

Who he wished to unlock
And lock its gate,
Who would cut the God-given earth
With a plough as if it were bread.

I know a nest, I like it much.
It warms me day and night,
Covered by the soft speech of mothers
And the hard work of fathers.

My good God, look down on it.
Guard it for us always.
O, great God, at least protect that
Which you made so small.

The walk arround
our beloved country has come
to the end. Perhaps you have
learned something new, or
missed something you know well,
and you think that others should
know it. It is always so when
there is not enough space. Everything you have found in this slim
little book was collected out of love
for the Slovak people and land. If
you take and mix a little history, some
places of interest, a pinch of the present,
and add to it a generous measure of love and
respect for the country, natural environment and
people, the overall result should be appetizing. The
Slovaks have always welcomed their guests with bread
and salt, in peace. We end our little book with a picture
of the high mountains which guard our homeland, with
a loaf of bread which tastes best at home, and a wish of
a full measure of happiness for our country and the
people who live in it, or whose ancestors came from it.